Mere Words On A Page

OBTAINING THE PROMISES OF GOD TO YOU

TO: Zeigler

May these words stir your heart in
The power of The Holy Spirit.
Apostle Craig —

Apostle Craig N. Wells

ROCWELLS PUBLISHING
P.O. BOX 490
SLIDELL, LOUISIANA 70459

1st *Printing*

Mere Words on a Page
Obtaining the promises of the Lord to You
ISBN 0-9740067-0-X

Copyright © 2003 by Craig N. Wells
Rock World Ministries
P.O. Box 490
Slidell, Louisiana 70459

Cover Design by Kimberly Archer
Edited by Tammy Gaines
Drafted by Michele Schwarz

Published by ROCWells Publishing
P.O. Box 490
Slidell, Louisiana 70459

Website: *www.rockworldministries.com*

Contents

Acknowledgements

I would like to give special thanks to Michele Schwarz for her endless hours of work and labor of love on this project. I also would like to thank her husband, Leo Schwarz, for sacrificing his wife's time to accomplish this project. Your family's gifts of time and love to this ministry have been done with excellence and outstanding efforts. We love you and thank you for this. Michele, thank you once again for giving us your talents and works of love...

Also, I would like to thank Pastor Tammy Gaines for her endeavoring efforts to proofread and edit this project and for helping make it a wonderful success.

My thanks go out to Kimberly Archer for donating her time and efforts for her work (graphics and design) on our beautiful cover.

Thanks to you both, Minister Tyrone and Rachelle Potts, for connecting us in the publishing field.

I would also like to thank my wife, Tina A. Wells, for pushing me as well as standing behind me to finish this project.

Apostle Aaron Smith, thank you for writing the forward to this book.

Most of all, I would like to thank and honor the Lord our God Most High, His Son Jesus the Christ, and the awesome friend of the Holy Spirit, for without You, none of this could be possible. But in Christ Jesus all things are possible. Thank you Father !

For our God is God...

Dedication

I would like to dedicate this book to my beautiful wife, Tina Anne Wells, whom I love with all my heart and my three wonderful children: Jeremy Nathaniel Wells, Jennifer Marie Wells, and Ashley Lynn Wells. They have supported me with all of their hearts and faith in this project as well as in many, many years of ministry.

There are so many others I would like to dedicate this book to. My Mom, Dorothy Neitschman, and my stepfather, Bob Neitschman, who never gave up on me. Thank you! My mom always buys the first thing I ever sell or create. She always wanted to be the first to make an investment in my life. I also want to thank my Dad, Alfred Wells, and my stepmom, Delores Wells, for under-girding this ministry and believing in me and the Word of the Lord in my life. I appreciate greatly all four of my parents for the action of their faith and believing in the Word of the Lord. All of you have stood together with me in defeating the enemy. And this has brought forth much fruit.

I want to dedicate this book also to my cousin, Pastor Steve and his wife, Beverly Vangeison, for always being friends beyond friends and encouraging me on this endeavor.

I also want to dedicate this project to Pastor/Prophet Thomas Gaines and his wife, Pastor Tammy Gaines of the Rock Church of Greater New Orleans. They have walked side-by-side with me in this ministry, working together to make this come to pass.

To my brother, Willis Wells, this book goes out

to you, too. I appreciate all of your love and prayers for me.

And this dedication goes out to my best friend, Andy and his wife, Teresa Glenn, who have always believed in me and the Word of the Lord in my life.

This dedication is also for the people of the Rock Church of Greater New Orleans, (Slidell, LA.) for as one body stands together, we will see the glory of God fill the earth, one person at a time.

To my Pastor, Apostle Aaron Smith and his wife, Pastor Robbie Smith, of the Rock of Mobile in Alabama, I dedicate this project. Your willingness to establish me and my family in the ministry of the Lord Jesus Christ and being a spiritual father that cared enough to make a difference means the world to me. Once again, I will proclaim that in every "No" you ever said to me, there was life.

Forward

I believe that without a doubt **religion** is the greatest tool that Satan, our enemy, uses to make the Word of God of no effect in our lives. Some think that when you say "***I'm religious***," it means that you have a relationship with God. This is simply not true. A religious spirit, in a sly way, waters down the Word of God that it would not be effective in our present-day life. Religion says the Word of God was effective yesterday - far, far behind us. It also says it will be available for us in the future, but never right now. The Scripture says the Word of God is living, powerful and sharper than any two-edged sword.

In the following pages, Apostle Craig Wells, in his own New Orleans flair, has greatly challenged us to see the Word of God as it is meant to be. To me, the most effective books are those written by someone with more than just a good idea. Apostle Craig has personally heard and applied what you're about to read. I know this, because as his apostle, I know the path which he has walked.

It's my understanding that he started this book halfway through the 8-year process of training to be the overcomer he is today. I must tell you that I know Craig lived in a battle to obtain the promises of the Word of God. I know there were many days of struggle, but he would not quit because he truly believes the Word of God is for him and it's meant for now. If you will read this book and allow the words to come alive in your heart, you will obtain the promises for your life as well.

Apostle Aaron Smith
The Rock Ministries
Mobile, Alabama

Forward

There are times in our lives while serving the Lord that we receive words that do not seep immediately into our spirits. They seem to be superficial at best, and we understand them with our natural understanding but have no revelation truth to back them up. These are the words that we must meditate on and rehearse in order for God to reveal to us the true meaning behind them. Apostle Craig has taken simple truths that we've all heard over the years, but may have only understood with our minds, and brought revelation truth to them. He has meditated on them, and through Holy Spirit, been able to take profound, yet simple words, and explain them in a way that is easily understood. I would recommend this book to ministers and lay people alike for this book reminds us that God's Word is true and everlasting.

Pastor Tommy Gaines
The Rock Church
Slidell, LA 70459

This book by Apostle Craig N. Wells will help anyone walk out the Word of the Lord in their lives, whether it be the spoken Word or the written Word (the Bible). He both encourages and challenges us to receive that Word and believe it until it comes to pass. Also, Apostle Craig emphasizes the importance and significance of an intimate relationship with the Father. Surely, you will see by reading this book that the Word of God is not just ***"mere words on a page."***

Pastor Tammy Gaines
The Rock Church
Slidell, LA 70459

Forward

Under the unction of the Holy Ghost I was led to pen truths about the author, Apostle Craig N. Wells and his wonderful family whom I love very much. When we met, I perceived in my spirit that he was a man sold out and on fire for Jesus, a man of vision and a man being used mightily by God for His glory! I knew immediately he was of a five-fold ministry, faith and spirit-filled and hailed out of a covering greater than him. As I grew to know Apostle and First Lady Wells, I realized they were both humble people of God who have a love for our region and the world. They love God with all their hearts and impart and dispense to all who will receive fresh oil and new wine into their lives. This is why we connect. We see both the new day that is here and a greater dispensation of a new day that is approaching us.

Apostle Wells knows we must be a "biblically" wise and prepared people if we're to reap the blessings and benefits of knowing and having God as Father. God said in His most Holy Word, "*I would not have my people ignorant.*" The ministry of Apostle Wells and the Rock Church are founded on hearing and obeying the Holy Spirit and the Word of the Lord. They have been sent to our region by God for the advancement and establishment of the Kingdom of God. He is reaching out to the spiritual, physical and emotional needs of the people of our community with the love of Jesus Christ and the power of the Holy Spirit. Apostle Wells flows freely in every five-fold ministry gift and God is raising him to provide a ministry to families where they can be planted and grow to the fullness of the plan of God's destiny for their lives. Apostle and First Lady Wells strive for excellence in every area of their lives. He is a great prophet, priest and king over his home and lives the life he preaches and teaches about. The Spirit of the Lord God is definitely upon him.

*"**Mere Words on a Page**"* is an awesome witness and testimony declaring that our God is an awesome God and His Word is His Will for our lives today and always has been. All who read this great book will obtain 'mere wisdom from God.' God's Word teaches us the more excellent way for living and it also teaches correction and gives instruction. This book is a powerful tool inspired by God to bless His people in every area of their lives. I salute you, Apostle Wells, for your awesome accomplishment of placing pen to parchment and allowing the Holy Spirit to guide you in writing in this new era, a Number 1 best seller that will give divine revelation and inspiration to God's people. It will challenge them to seek God diligently and faithfully, always obeying Him, always pursuing a better relationship with God and knowing how to apply His Word to their lives daily. They will be able to reap the promises of God to overflowing and to be a blessing until all the nations of the world are blessed. Continue to place pen to parchment, Apostle, and God will give you the unction and inspiration. *"**Mere Words on a Page**"* is a MUST READ for the Third Day Church.

Prophetess Kathleen Javery-Bacon
Holy Ghost and Fire Revival Ministries International
Slidell, Louisiana

Preface

This book is **dangerously challenging**, yet "***simple but profound***". You will need to read it multiple times to unlock the hidden mysteries of God in these pages before you. You have the ability to be changed into God's armor guard and by faith, nothing will be able to stand in your way of obtaining the promises of God in your life. Are you telling me that there is a formula to getting all your needs and wants from God? Of course, my answer will be, "No!" People are always looking for a formula or guideline to get to heaven or to what heaven offers to us. Many before me as well as many after me may try to sell you this process, formula, or seven-step plan. But I am here to relieve you of all of that mess. Formulas, steps, and plans are always about a way we can reach God on our own, but in all reality, He has already made a way for you and me to receive all that we need from Him.

It's not about a goal of obtaining our promises. We may think if we get good enough or do enough, just maybe we can prove ourselves to the Lord in this. And if that's not our reasoning, maybe we look at these one, two, three steps of reaching God on our own as a way we may seem acceptable to Him. Or maybe we want an easier way out than dealing with the truth of what all the Father really wants and longs for us to have. All that it takes is for you and I to have a deep, intimate relationship with King Jesus, where He takes the utmost precedence in our life. It's not in religion or law but in relationship.

So, you will not find a formula or get-it-quick scheme to realize your goal before God; just a simple message of love from the Father of what He is willing to do for those that are willing to commit and see it through to the end is what you will find. Then, you will reap the rewards of the Kingdom in your life. I declare to you that the Father is wanting you to be His glory in the earth and that there is nothing that He will hold back from His own. *So arise sons and daughters of the Most-High God and take your place in this time and in this land and conquer what God has set before you*. For the Spirit of the Lord is moving over all of the earth looking and longing to show Himself mighty on your behalf. I ask you this day, *will you be the one?* Will you be the place of habitation that the Father will show up greatly in? Come with me as we enter into this book on a journey of truth and life and the pursuit of God's promises , the utmost pursuit of the Most-High God...

For Our God Is God

CHAPTER ONE

Introduction
Why Mere Words on a Page

"Uugh!!! *What is this?,"* I exclaimed. I yelled this **"uugh"** out in pain. As this was happening, I thought about a cartoon character that I had watched when I was younger. Charlie Brown is his name. He would see Lucy with that ball. She would lift it up as if she really wanted him to kick the field goal and she would taunt him with it. "Come on and kick, Charlie Brown. You can do it. Come on, kick that ball right through the goal. I won't move it," she exclaimed. Lucy had done this so many times before. The temptation for him to believe her was overwhelming. Finally, you guessed it, he went for it. Away Charlie Brown went, running as fast as he could. When he went to kick the football, as always, Lucy pulled it away and Charlie Brown flew through the air. He flew through the air with so much grief and despair that he landed on his butt howling, **"Uugh"**, very loudly. Now that he had believed Lucy, he felt the pain and embarrassment because what she said were just *"mere words on a page."* What she said was nothing to be believed. It was just some hope or dream gone by or a simple wish on a star gone sour.

That's how I felt about life and God's Word as I began to write this book. I felt a huge **"Uugh!"** Is it really what I believe? Are the things written in God's Word really true? Is it really for me or are they just mere words on a page? What is it all about?

You may be asking the same questions. "What is it all about? Are they just mere words on a page?" I don't have a magical answer or some quick solution for life and its problems. No "**Hocus-pocus**," "**Alacazam**," or even "**AbraCadabra**" will do the trick. Some may say, as if they have some kind of magic wand in the sky, that when they use the name of Jesus, problems disappear. The problem, for the most part, will not just go away by saying, "In Jesus' Name." That doesn't make everything better because if it did, we'd all wake up in the morning and everything would be perfect.

Well, didn't that preacher say all I had to do is say "Jesus"? What's up with this? I guess it doesn't work for me. It sure looks like it is working for the preacher. Is he reading out of a special book or is it the same Bible I have? Well, I guess it just won't work for me. It's simply words of a good sermon. Have you, yes you, ever felt like Charlie Brown?

"Let's go," the preacher exclaimed. The crowd yelled "**Amen!**" He holds the whole world in His hands. You are like little grains of sand that he holds. He has it all under control. He shouts and the people say "**Amen**" again. You felt His voice, you hear his words, warm feelings of joy do flood you, and you agree in your heart. He quotes scriptures that bring you joy and even a heart-felt prayer that brings a tear to your eyes. You are shouting and agreeing with this man and his words.

Back to home you go. At first the joy still surrounds you as you begin to make dinner. By 6 p.m., you're tired and the kids are running around. The television is blaring. Now it's time to go to sleep. Quickly you reflect and think about the words you heard that day. You wake up in the morning feeling, 'Oh it's just another day.' What happened to the joy, the shout, the peace you felt? Man, at the end of the sermon, you were on your knees weeping with joy. By now another day has come and gone and you have forgotten the words you've heard. Inside yourself you now wonder what was it he said, was any of it really true, and if it was, why is it not happening to me. Mere words that sound so full of life but by now, three days later, you're still living in strife. What shall you do? You really wanted to believe His words were true. By now, maybe you see yourself in the middle of this page going through some kind of trouble or problem that just won't go away.

This could be a hidden "**sin**". Wow, he didn't use that word, did he? Yes, "**sin**," not to condemn but also not to just let it slide by because we have not yet been able to overcome it. And you have heard the Word, read the Word, spoke the Word, and claimed the Word. Somehow, over a period of time, that problem, trouble, illness, desire, or that hidden sin just got too big. Just like Humpty Dumpty when all the King's horses and all the King's men couldn't put him back together again, that is where it seems we stand. We are broken in pieces, fallen from our place, uprooted or cast down, crushed in our state of being. We are just flat, out-right defeated. And we wonder, "What about the book, the words of a man, all of life's goals and every one of my plans? They sometimes seem so far away! **Words, Words, Words, is that all there is or is there more?"**

Well some of you can't relate or you're not willing to admit you've been living a life that just doesn't add up to what the preacher says or what the Bible says. This must be the way God planned it: this one is sick or maybe diseased , this one living in poverty, or this one seems to be living under a curse. Maybe someone died way before his time and you're thinking that this must be God's will. You know, the Lord knows! That's right, the Lord knows. Maybe everything in your life seems okay. Maybe you're not ever daring to challenge your life by the Words of the Book. Maybe you just take life for granted believing this is the way things must be. But your life is not adding up to what the preacher says on television. **Mere words on a page! Yes, Mere words on a page?** I wonder how this could be; I never looked at my life in the reflection of those words to see what I could see. What a thought that one may believe, those mere words on a page are all for him to receive.

What about this, could all this be true? Should I look at my life in the reflection of those words, or the Sunday School lesson I heard? Should I just take things as they are to be because this is the way life is going for me? Wow, what a thought! If this is you, go ahead and grab your chair and hang on for the ride. This book will change your life and make you think in a new way: like Christ. The word says, "**Have this mind in you**." What mind? The mind of Christ, so agree with me that as you read this book, He is setting you free to find out His Word and all of His promises for you. They're not just *mere words on a page.*

Psalm 105:19 Until the time of the word came: the word of the Lord tried him.

Remember: It is not the man that hears the word of the Lord only, but it is unto the one that will obey that word and walk out the process of that word all the way to the end of fulfillment . It is he that will receive the prize.

James 1:12 Blessed (happy, to be envied) is the man who is patient under trial and stands up under temptation, for when he has stood the test and been approved, he will receive (the victor's) crown of life Which God has promised to those who love Him.

Remember: You are on a mission from the Lord, not to be taken likely or to be easily looked upon.
The Master's call to prosper you and to fulfill His plan in your life is a serious undertaking by God and man.

In every dream and Hope before God is the power to make one be or the disappointment to destroy one's beliefs, it's your decision
not to be moved. ***Believe to the end.***

CHAPTER TWO

All My Tomorrows Vs. All My Sorrows

Have you ever felt like just giving up, not going on anymore? Maybe you don't have the strength in you. Thoughts that say, "I hate my life," or "This situation is way too much for me," or "I just can't take it anymore!" You look at your life and begin to wonder what it's all about. What am I here for? Or maybe you are holding on to regrets: If I would only have married him, or if I would have gotten this certain education I would be better now, or if my family would have done this or given me that, or if my dad and mom would have loved me more. I sure wish I would have not gained so much weight, maybe people would love me then. Or you look back when you were a child and hurts begin to flood your mind. You might look back and remember great memories about your childhood, but that's all gone now. Well, I know I'll better myself looking at all the hurts and pains of yesterday and building off of that. I'll know not to make any of those mistakes again.

Before I bring you deeper into this book, I want to jog your memory only for a moment so we can get it out of the way and never to go to that place again. But for right now, I feel we should look at it. You say look at what. Look at the pain, the trouble, the shame or maybe even the triumph of the victory that you hold on to. Consciously or unconsciously, I know you're saying, "What does this have to do with the Word of the Lord and its power or lack of power in my life?" As these pages unfold, you will see. This picture of your sorrows has affected the very power of God's Word in your life, even in some cases, to no avail. So let's look back at our past just for this moment. You see it's so easy to look at our future or our goals. 'Yes, I want to be this or maybe that. I will climb to this height in my life and find peace.' Well that might all be true but where are you today? Why are you bound in some things in your life, right now, that won't seem to let go? You say, "Oh no, not me". Let's be completely honest with ourselves right now and begin to take inventory. Don't put yourself down or think that you're a dirty, rotten sinner. Let me help you out with that one. You are not! You are a blood-bought, saved from the wages of sin, cleansed from head to toe, temple of the Holy Ghost where God Almighty lives. He paid a great price for you. So you tell yourself, even in the state that you are in, as we look back at our past for a moment that you are a precious gem, a fine costly jewel. You are more valuable than anything to Him. He was willing to pay the price, not on credit. There is no debt carried over your head. You have become debtless or debt free to sin by Christ. That is awesome! That means you are free. This is another subject we will be getting into as we go along in this book.

But now as you are excited about being free, let's go to yesterday, only for this moment. When I was a little boy, I used to work in the cafeteria at lunch time. I helped out as a dishwasher. Some people thought that was a demeaning job, not me.

You see if you worked in the kitchen, you could get all the lunch you wanted for free. What a reward that was to me, even though at the time I was skin and bones. I was the one taking full benefit of that reward!

Now I'm a little older, and I don't need any of those types of benefits anymore, eating all I want, if you know what I mean. It reminds me of a poster that I saw everyday in the cafeteria hall that I wish would have taken more notice of. It said, "You are what you eat." Wow, when I look in the mirror, somehow I can really remember that poster. Who knew how true that saying really was? Well, let's look at that for a moment. You are what you eat. What about how we think about our future in the sight of our past. Now can you see where I am getting?

So let's look truthfully and clearly, just you and I, so nobody else has to know. No, I'm not looking into your mind so I won't tell. Let's dig deep for a moment. Could it be nobody ever loved you like you wanted to be loved, or you did not make the dance team in school? Maybe you were too afraid of failure so you never tried out for the dance team or football team. Maybe your first love took your heart and your virginity and never gave it back. You could have been the school geek that everybody made fun of or you were the super jock that was the all sport leader but now you can't even keep a wife. It could be a promise that never was fulfilled or one or too many dreams that never came true. Was it a victory that you're still holding on to, but now, there are no new victories to shout about? You're now saying, "What is this writer getting to? Where is he going? I don't see myself in any of those words." Well, look deeper into your own heart and pinpoint those things that might be lying there. Super victories may be there but more likely, super hurts or even some kind of abuse. You might even think everything's fine. You had great parents, a wonderful time in school, college was awesome, and now your career is doing just fine. And that well may be true for a lot of us, too. I have found that where I'm taking you, none of it, even the good, can go where we are going. It's kind of like going through the eye of the needle. All of it, not lacking one bit, whatever we have clothed ourselves with must be shed: pain, hurt, bad memories, regrets, victories, or triumphs. Some of you might say, "I don't want to let go of that or this was good. I don't want to set that aside. Wait a minute. That trophy badge that I wear over my head as a shield, it protects me. That's what I'm all about. I did those things or accomplished those victories."

On the other spectrum, "He hurt me. They didn't really like me or nobody let me be me. I'm not worth much. All I ever do is fail and that's just the way it's going to be." Deep inside, you really hate yourself, wishing the pain would go away from a life you never wanted anyway. Oh, I wish that never would have happened. Oh if I just would have done this. I'm sure if this one wanted me, it would have been different. It could be victories you're not willing to let go of. I remember when I took my high school team to this victory or I was the best singer in my Sunday School. I only got A's in school. Better yet, everybody always liked me in college. I was voted most likely to succeed. **Blah, Blah, Blah, Blah, Blah.** No, I'm not trying to belittle your victories or make fun of your pain but we must lay them down. We need to shed the garments of our successes and failures, like dirty clothes and step through the eye of the needle. Some of you are saying, "What, take off my garments, I'll be naked. I've been wearing these old things for so-so long. I can't. I'll be vulnerable and I don't know what I'll do without them." They may be as some baby blanket for comfort that seem to bring life. They're really garments of chains and heavy weights just holding you down. You might even be the one saying that you're not going to let go. The only problem is they're wrapped around your neck, choking out the new life that wants to come in. I'm not saying you have to forget them. I have lots of good, even great memories. As a Christian your life should be filled with great memories.

I'm saying it's time that we don't wear them anymore. Come clean, naked before our Lord. Shed all of the hurts, victories, sins and joys and go on through His eye of the needle so we can become clean of ourselves and renewed unto him, full of His glory. Go ahead right now. There's no need to wait until the end of the book. Just for this moment, stop reading, think on those things of the past. Look deeply into what you've been wearing. You know you can't wear two sets of garments at one time or else it will be most constricting and uncomfortable. Now the Word says, **"Put on the whole armor of God: Helmet of Salvation, Breastplate of Righteousness, Sword of the Spirit, Shield of Faith, your feet shod with preparation of the Gospel, your loins girded with Truth.** (Eph. 1:7-14). How can you put these things on if you are already clothed with your own garments such as: Breastplate of Pride, Helmet of Sorrow, feet full of confusion, loins dipped in lies, Shield of Hurt and the Sword of Despair? You could even be clothed in the might of old victories gone by, so right now, let's get past our sorrows, victories and pain, and get naked before our God.

You've always wondered why sometimes you get so beat up in the battle and it seems to hurt so badly. It's because your new garments of protection don't fit well over your garments of pain and pride. They keep falling off or they are not covering all they need to. But if you get naked before our King, pass through the eye of His needle and take off all of you, He will clothe you in Righteousness. This righteousness will be able to withstand all the wiles of the devil and you will stand in His Victory. So, are you ready? I wish music were playing but it's a book so I can't add music.

Well in your mind right now, go ahead, play some form of royal music. Act as if a knight were about to be crowned with the honor from a King, trumpets are blowing, fanfare is in the air, wind is blowing of His glory all around you. Angels are bowing and singing, **"Holy is the Lamb."** You are now in the presence of the Almighty God, the True King. So off go your shoes of the path you've taken so far. Now unveiled are your loins of intimacy that you have shared with so many pains and also with victories you have won. Now off goes the breastplate of pride you've held to so true. Laying down your own sword, you know this you must do. Now off go your shield so battered and torn and your old beat up helmet you have so proudly worn. Oh you are free, free! Hear the angels cheer as you begin to feel the presence of God and draw near to His throne. At first you are afraid of what He might see but as you get closer, His eyes are full of love for thee. You begin to feel as one in a drunken stupor as the presence of God covers you. Finally to the stairs, you are looking up toward the throne with thoughts racing through your head, "This is not where I belong." You want to turn and run because you have not been here before. But a voice of thunder rings in your ear, "Come closer, closer, my child. I want to see, I want to hold you in my arms and get really close to thee." For a moment your mind begins to refute and say, "No, not me. Look at what you see," forgetting that now you are naked and all that is left is thee. "My child, my child, you are my Holy one, I bought and paid for you through the redemption of my Son. So come here, get closer, get off of your bended knee. I've been waiting for you all this time, just to get close to thee. For I love you with an everlasting love and now I'm setting you free to wear the garments, so full of life: first the Helmet of Salvation. Now I put it on your head that you will never stray. Now let me gird your loins with my truth in you as I put the fire of My

Spirit deep inside of you. Armor plate for battle, on your chest it goes but I've already won the war. So know this, as you fight my righteousness will turn back the Devil at every stand and he will bow down to you at every command. So quickly I put My shoes on you, wrapped and tied and bound, the Gospel of My Son would lead you to where you should be found. Now you are ready for My sword. It is My Word. It is in your mouth, speak it bold, and speak it loud. Never mix it with doubt. Hold fast to this Shield of Faith, in it you withstand. For every promise you see fulfilled will be by its command. So you're all dressed up and ready to go. I knight thee King and Priest and may the rule of your domain in Me upon you never cease."

Right now receive His true armor. It's not some scripture we read or some simple step to follow, it's the armor of God. But we press through, laying down and aside all our sorrows that, we may conquer in Him for all of our tomorrows. **Ephesians 1:7-8** says, *"In Him* **(Christ " the anointed")** *we* **(meaning you and me)** *have redemption through His blood, the total* **(completely)** *forgiveness of sin, to be remembered no more by the Father, otherwise, a complete pardon, guiltless, according to the riches of His grace, which He made to abound toward us in all wisdom and prudence,* **Ephesians 1:13.** *In Him you also trusted: after you heard the word of truth, the Gospel of your salvation in whom also having believed you were sealed with the Holy Spirit of*

promise.

Wow, what a promise! To be sealed with His (God's) Holy Spirit is an awesome promise. Go ahead right now and reaffirm your faith in His word and declare, "I am saved and filled with Holy Spirit by the promise of the Father in Jesus Christ." Wow, listen to what God's Word has to say about the promises of the seal which is the Holy Spirit. **Ephesians 1:14** *Who is (meaning Holy Spirit) the guarantee of the inheritance, until the redemption of the purchased possessions to the praise of His Glory.* Now let's take a look at that. You have been sealed by Holy Spirit, redeemed (to be made new) by His blood and set free from all of your yesterdays, ungirded and brought before Him, only to be made clean and called son or daughters of the Most High God. This is an awesome truth that you need to remind yourself of every day. You are a new creature in Christ, today. God is a God of the Now. He is chasing and changing lives now. I don't know about you, but such excitement and joy comes to my heart when I think about what you are reading in this chapter. Take a journey away from your old hurts and pains and lay them down at the feet of Jesus. That way you are called sons or daughters of the Most High God without shame. His love toward you is full of grace, mercy, and love and it is cleansing you. He is dressing you with His armor, not to be taken off. Then he knights you kings and priests, then gives you the seal of the promise, the baptism of the Holy Spirit. This is about shouting time!

Be free in Jesus' Name! Right now, I release freedom in your life to let go of those old garments so you may take on His. In Jesus' Name, be thou made whole. Well shout, somebody! You're going to heaven and the devil can't do anything about it. You're going to obtain all of the promises that God has for you, right here on earth, in your lifetime, because He has a plan for you. Now your old garments won't get in the way and you will win the battle. Now you are battle-dressed, full of His armor. He baptized you full of the seal of the promise, the Holy Spirit. Glory be to God! You had better watch out. This book is powerful. Go ahead and expect to be changed, to be different and to be empowered by God. By the time you get finished reading, you will be cleaned and free. What a thought! You might be saying, "Wait a minute, I've been saved. I've already received the promise of the Holy Spirit. What changes did those words I just read make in me?"

Don't get me wrong, I'm not saying that you were not a Christian before you read those pages or that you were not full of the Holy Ghost. I'm saying, "Renew yourself." Your past is redeemed unto God; those old garments are gone now. Reaffirm your love for Him and the gift of the promise, the Holy Spirit. Get naked before God. Come clean and get knighted all over again. Be fresh and full of the power of His love for you. It's kind of like a marriage, after the honeymoon, you take your course on down the road. Over a period of time, baggage and luggage of all kinds (hurt, disappointment, pain, jealousy, etc.) begin to come along for the trip. Go back to a place of Holy Communion where you both come clean and start afresh in each other's eyes. Your marriage would soon die and you would get bored or you would become distant from each other without that fresh, clear intimacy. So let this become as you and the Father are today: clean, fresh, empowered with Him. Old things, even those experiences since you became born again, are now passed away and behold, you are new kings and priests before the Lord. You have become ready, willing, and able to receive all of the promises of our great God. Glory to His Holy Name! For He will perform His Word to you as you hold on, press in and begin to know yourself and see yourself as our Heavenly Father sees and knows you. Then you will arise as a strong mighty unmovable man/woman of God, prepared to do great exploits for our awesome King Jesus. Arise sons and daughters of God and be His Glory and His Strength in the earth.

Psalms 139:1-18   O LORD, you have searched me (thoroughly) and have known me. You know my downsitting and my uprising; You understand my thought afar off. You sift and search out my path and my lying down and You are acquainted with all my ways. For there is not a word in my tongue (still uttered), but, behold, O Lord, You know it altogether. You have beset me and shut me in- behind and before, and You have laid Your hand upon me. Your (infinite) knowledge is too wonderful for me; it is high above me, I cannot reach it. Where could I go from Your Spirit? Or where could I flee from Your presence? If I ascend up into heaven, You are there; if I make my bed in Sheol (the place of the dead), behold, You are there. If I take the wings of the morning or dwell in the uttermost parts of the sea, Even there shall Your hand lead me, and Your right hand shall hold me. If I say, Surely the darkness shall cover me and the night shall be (the only) light about me, Even the darkness hides nothing from You, but the night shines as the day; the darkness and the light are both alike to You. For You did form my inward parts; You did knit me together in my mother's womb. I will confess and praise You for You are fearful and wonderful and for the awful wonder of my birth! Wonderful are Your works, and that my inner self knows right well. My frame was not hidden from You when I was being formed in secret (and) intricately and curiously wrought (as if embroidered with various colors) in the depths of the earth (a region of darkness and mystery). Your eyes saw my unformed substance, and in Your book all the days (of my life) were written before ever they took shape, when as yet there was none of them. How precious and weighty also are Your thoughts to me, O God! How vast is the sum of them! If I could count them, they would be more in number than the sand. When I awoke, (could I count to the end) I would still be with you.

If I have learned anything in the 28 years of serving the Lord Most High, is that it does not matter what you go through He will always be there. In most cases waiting for us to call on Him, but His love for you will never ever fail. It is from everlasting to everlasting. That's right even you, whatever you are going through you may call him right this very second. I don't care how you feel or what you think you have done to miss the plan of God, our God in His awesomeness is waiting for you to call on Him and receive His love and mercy so that you may cry out like King David did so many times in Psalms. " Father your mercy endureth forever." I am not justifying any of your sins or mistakes or mishaps in your life, but I can promise you one thing ,t Jesus Christ is the Veto of your sins or your pain or even your failures and He sets you free.

CHAPTER THREE

From Now Until Then

Well, I know you have enjoyed the first chapter and by now you are hungry for more. So let's get right into things that we need in our lives to fulfill what God has for us. "Mere Words on a Page," what does that really mean? Well basically, it means that all the words that the preacher has been preaching, or the prophet has been prophesying, or even the Words of the Bible that have not been fulfilled seem like mere words on a page. Over the years, you haven't seen enough changes and the promises you thought were true never came to pass. Well, we are going to remedy that. Now that we have come clean before the Lord, we are going to begin to build the new man again. Repeat this with me. ***"The Word of the Lord shall come true to me. The Father will perform His work in me. My destiny will be fulfilled."***

We are going to empty out and then refill your mind, soul, and spirit with an empowered Word of God. No more thinking about promises unfulfilled or hopes that have been banished. No more thinking about some great sermon that you really believed was true but it really did not do anything for you. Your life is basically the same as it was last year. Now all of that is going to change. You say, Apostle Craig, that sure is a big order. I've read the Word, I've heard the preaching, I've gotten the tapes and videos, but my situation has never changed. I'm still in Hopeville, never ever seeming to get the truth of the Word into my reality, and that sickness just doesn't seem to know God's Word. My poverty doesn't seem like it will ever realize I'm a child of God. My children seem they'll never get saved and I know too many loved ones that have gone to the grave in hope of their salvation. Some just die too soon or realize too late. Through all of my hopes and my dreams, I know I stand on the Word of the Lord, but tomorrow when I wake up it's still all the same.

So my word to you my friend is equip yourself for battle, take the world at your command. Now you're saying, I thought I did that in the last chapter, taking on His armor. Well don't get me wrong, that was right and great but there is more. A soldier does not just get dressed for battle, He must get equipped for battle and that we are going to do in this chapter.

The Word says, *"Not by might, nor by power, but by My Spirit says the Lord."* Now let's think on that for a minute. For too many of us Christians, this is a familiar and simple scripture. It is taken way too lightly. Sometimes we find ourselves, as born again believers, full of head knowledge, quoting scriptures randomly and carelessly. *"Not by might, nor by power, but by the Spirit of the Lord"*, or *"My God shall supply all my needs"*, or *"Give and it shall be given pressed down, shaken together, and running over."* Maybe even, *"For God so loved the world that He gave His only Begotten Son."* Whatever the scripture is, somehow over a period of time, many of these beloved scriptures lose its zing in your ear. You just say them, regretfully, and most often powerlessly. Could it be you are quoting it to a friend in need, or a problem in your life, or just saying it in a prayer? You know how to remind God of His Word. Oh don't get me wrong, it is okay to pray scriptures.

When Jesus was here on earth He quoted scriptures all the time. But He was also the fulfillment of the verse He quoted. When you are quoting scripture in your prayer it's not for God, it is for you, to give you something to stand on. But does it? Are those Words really real to you? Do you know even as Christ Jesus was the fulfillment of these scriptures, and as He spoke those words, things happened. They were real and alive. They were changing His World around Him. Also everyone He was around was being changed by those words. This too is true of you. You are the fulfillment of God's Word today. God said in His Word, heaven and earth will pass away but my Word will stand forever. Forever, that means from way in the past to way in the future. That Word that you take in your mouth and speak out sometimes so loosely and that seems so powerless as it drops to the ground before your problem and your problem is still there, that same Word is the Word of God. Really, it is Jesus in the form of the Word.

The Bible said in John 1:1 that **the Word became flesh (Jesus Christ).** **He was from the beginning and all things were made by Him.** What do we do sometimes with that Word, quote or throw it around like a loose cannon at our enemies?

Sometimes we even use it on our friends to get our way or at our husband or at our wife to fight a battle or to prove a point. We can make it useless and undermining of what that Word is really there for. It's kind of like bringing a cannon to a water gun fight. Its use is not for its intended purpose. That purpose is to bring life. I said "life" is the intended purpose of that Word in your mouth. When using the Word with people, is it to bring life to people or just to bring a victory to your side of the problem or cause? Let's go back to what I said in the paragraph before, Jesus Christ was the fulfillment of scripture and I'm sure in your minds, you all said "**Amen**." We agree, He was and is awesome.

Now let's go to, "**You are the fulfillment of scripture**." Let us digest that for a moment. Do you feel the same way about that saying as you did when I said, **"Jesus is the fulfillment of Scripture."**? I know you could see Jesus Christ, the anointed Son of God, full of glory and power, Holy and righteous in all of His life, surely He is the fulfillment. But you, yes you, you are the adopted son/daughter of the living God through Christ Jesus. It said in His Word you are the righteousness of God in Christ Jesus, **you're it**. Now come to the battlefield with that knowledge. Know that you being flesh, it is no more you but the one inside of you who has made you free from the bondage of sin. He has brought you into His marvelous light. You are the temple of His Holy Spirit and carrier of His Holy Word. You have been washed and have been made clean and accepted by God. Now you have become the Word in fulfillment through Christ. By the power of the Holy Spirit working inside of you, you have an arsenal of word weapons in you. They must be used for their intended use so they can accomplish all that He has for them. What do you mean "intended use"? I thought I just remembered scripture and quoted them at will and somehow it made me more of a Christian. If I could quote lots of Scriptures, I thought it made a difference but sometimes it really doesn't.

Just reading the Bible and rolling out a scripture and quoting it at your situation is not always the way. Think of it kind of like fixing a car, you need a wrench with a 5/16 head, but you just reach in and grab out any wrench. It probably won't fit and it will be harder and take a lot longer than it should have to fix it. Another example, you're a brain surgeon and you ask for a scalpel but you get out a chain saw, not too helpful. That's how it is if the right Word of the Lord is not used. Don't get me wrong, all Holy Scripture is the inspired Word of God. Scripture is true and powerful! It takes more than just grabbing the first thing out of your bag of goodies to fight the fight and to get the desired result. That's when the scriptures come in again. *"Not by might, nor by power, but by my Spirit,"* says the Lord. We must know our enemy and we must know our weapons. You would not bring a gun box full of guns to a gun fight and just show them off around the room while the enemy took aim at you and began to fire. No! We have got to dig into our Word, learn our weapons. It's not just some good scripture we turn into a song at church. It's not some scripture we heard our preacher say, or something we read in some evangelical magazine. We must know it by the spirit. The revelation of that Word must come true to us. Jesus could do all that He could do because He knew the Word. He was the Word. He was in such relationship with the Father that the Word was real and true and alive in Him. So He became a marksman of the Word and where He aimed it, it did go. It accomplished all that it was supposed to by the Spirit of the Living God. Now it's your turn to be that Word brought forth in the earth by the Spirit of God.

Be in relationship with your Heavenly Father and His Word and His Spirit that you are no longer spewing out words so aimlessly. They will be targeted words of the Lord that are just like heart-seeking missiles, able to divide asunder all that is in its way. All things around you will begin to line up as you get a hold of that Word, in which you are, the Word made real in the flesh by Jesus Christ through His Holy Spirit. Go ahead and take that to the bank, and get the Word of God in you. Allow Holy Spirit to reveal it to you and begin to stand on those words. See now if the gates of Hell itself can not prevail against you. Now when this revelation that you are the manifestation of the Word in the earth today gets in you, it will change all things around you and in you. Then you will bring out the right scripture gun for the battle and win the victory because you'll already know, the battle is not yours, it's the Lord's. It's been won! Really, you are supposed to be His expressed glory in the earth. His Word is going forth and is making today's man His sons in the earth. You're it. Climb into intimacy with that Word. Give birth to the Word, become the Word, become a powerful standard of Christ in the earth. See who you really are and how precious you really are to Him. Know that He would do anything to get you back to Himself. I'm sure the moment after man fell in the garden, God began to do all He could do to win His relationship back with man. That you could be His expressed image of His word on the earth is God's desire. He longed for it so badly that He was willing to sacrifice and send His only son, Jesus Christ, as the Word to be made manifest. He did this so that you and I could and would have relationship with Him and be His glory and to be His heir to all of His provision, all of His benefits and all that He has. You have obtained and you have become the Glory of God.

I'm sure by now all the angels in Heaven are rejoicing as they read this another time. It's brought to their memory that He's won. He's won the battle for His children and He did it all for you so He could get His Word in you and you would realize the glory and power and wonder of our God in your life here on earth. What an awesome God we have! He does love you and me. These thoughts of being the benefactor of His love are leaving me speechless. Just for a moment go ahead and give God the praise, right there where you are, for His love toward you. WOW!

His Word is everlasting and powerful in battle

and able to overturn the enemy in your life. It is able to change any situation, able to bring freedom and peace. But it must be first in you, a part of you, revealed to you out of revelation of the Spirit that you get out of your time with Him. Take it, wrap it about you, stand on it, digest it, become it. It has all that you need. It is life indeed, but it must become revelation to you, not just something you read. Make it who you are because you are the Word manifested in the earth. Devils tremble at what's inside of you. You come carrying the anointed Word of Almighty God. How many people would like to say they do that? Don't you realize you do? You are equipped for battle. But you are now also expected for celebration. It is time to rejoice in Him because it is already done, He's won. It is now time for you to agree in your heart and spirit. Please, don't let go, no matter what you see, until the manifestation comes through to your victory. So many times it seems as Christians we bring out our war fatigues uniform when really He wants us to bring out our dress blues. You see in the military their clothes for battle were camouflage army fatigues, clothes meant for combat. Then there is also a dress uniform, still a military soldier's uniform, but it's sharp and clean, shining with the awards of victory and meant for a celebration or banquet. I think we need to go ahead and put on our dress blues, shine up our metals of glory for God and celebrate His victory in the earth. Wear your walking and talking with confidence clothes. A great price was paid for you to wear it.

Not to be redundant, but sometimes we oversimplify the price that was paid on the cross. A man with feelings, hanging for hours on a tree by His arms and with nails that have been nailed there with spikes. To make things worse, He had just gotten a back beating with a whip so badly that He was not recognizable. Then, they crowned Him with a crown of thorns that stuck in His head and at last, pierced him with a spear in His side until the blood and water ran down His beaten body. All of this was done while He had all the power of Heaven in His hands. At any moment, He could have called down angels to destroy all that was around and set Him free. Many said the one who could heal and save so many couldn't even set Himself free, and you know they were right. All the power of God Himself is in the man, Jesus Christ. But He could not allow Himself to give in to the agony and pain or the malice and blasphemy of His name. He wanted to win you and me as His inheritance. He became the first seed of our redemption so we could be carriers of His seed, His Word.

We are His might and power in the earth. So gird up yourself in the relationship of His Word. Take on the image of our God and be like Him, the express manifestation of God in man on earth. Oh, what a price! Don't forget it; cherish it as a gift from the Lord. He took your place so you don't have to be defeated. You don't have to be sick or diseased; you don't have to live in turmoil or pain. You don't have to dwell in sin. You are an overcomer of this world, a mighty standard of His glory in the earth, through Jesus Christ and your relationship with the Father.

The Word said they overcome by the blood of the Lamb and the Word of their testimony. In Webster's dictionary, one of the definitions of testimony is "any form of evidence; proof." Is your life showing off any form of evidence or proof? Examine yourself against this Word. Surely the blood of the Lamb came as a gift. But we must live our life as one that is a living testimony of Him, evidence and proof of Him. May the end of our life prove to have been an overcoming life in Christ. So now we have come clean in Chapter one, encountered the Word as our choice weapon for life in Chapter two. As we go to Chapter four, prepare to be changed into His image and Glory.

CHAPTER FOUR

Let's Look a Little Deeper

Oh the joy to trust in Jesus, just to take Him at His Word. Wow, what a statement of faith , to only and completely trust in Jesus and to take Him at His Word. I am sure that you are like me and have found out that that is easier said than done. But don't forget the key to that statement, that I have just made, "easier said than done". Just because it is harder to do than to say does not mean that it does not get done. We must look deeper into the Word of God as well as deeper into our own hearts and belief system. For one moment, let's just make believe you are in one of my dynamic faith and healing filled services. I am just preaching away at the Word of God and it is awesome. (Bear with me a moment, I am not trying to make me sound great, I am painting a picture of a great church service where faith and power is released and then you and I will see what's next.)

Back in the service God is really moving, the worship is great, and the Word fits your every need. You are on your feet shouting and dancing unto your God in great jubilee and agreeing with what I am preaching to you under the anointing. But you leave the service and somehow within a day or so, you are still you, back in that same old situation that you had before the man of God preached a Word that you needed to hear. You were moved with faith to believe God for everything and anything (as it is right, you should), but somehow you are back to you.

Well, this is where you must look deeper into the whole picture. It is great to join your faith with another man or woman or even child of God, while they are teaching, preaching or praying. Most of the time you are hearing a Word of the Lord. You and I are hearing the end product, what happens after faith and the healing power of God completes the work. **There is a process.** This process is unexplainable by man or wisdom, or even by religious standards and guidelines that we seem to go by. 'But God,' here it is, is our only true salvation and He will make sure that we are firm on this one truth. 'But God,' that's right, but when God moves nothing or no one can stand before Him and His plan in your life. Even if you are like Joseph in the pit or jail cell, keep your eyes on Jesus and His Word to you and He will see you through. Sometimes the process is very, very unbearable but if you and I will hold on to the real truth that God is working everything out for our benefit, it will be easier. I don't care what your situation says or what trial you are going through, our Heavenly Father is an awesome God and He is desiring to work it out for you and cause you to be the victor. So you may say, "What are you saying, from now on don't go to one of those faith filled services." Of course not, but what I am saying is glean deeper into the Word that is coming forth and grab a hold of what the process is and allow it to have its perfect work in you. Know that it is your Heavenly Father that is really working in you. I am here to tell you that the Word of the Lord is standing true to you, even when it sometimes or maybe even all the time seems like it is not. My God and your God never, ever fails to him that will believe to the end. What an awesome God we serve!

He loves you and the answer is on the way. The Word of the Lord to you is more than just mere words on a page. They are the anointed Words of Almighty God. Please trust Him like never before, embrace the fire of God with joy and declare with all your heart and might that **"I WILL NOT BE DENIED."** God's Word will come to pass in my life for He who has called me is Faithful and true and everlasting love is upon me. My Father loves me. I don't care what you might have done in this life up until this point, I am telling you, through Christ Jesus and His shed blood covenant, you are forgiven. You are first spiritually made whole, the body and mind must follow. Be made whole and set free in Jesus' name right now. Say this with me, "My God loves me and He is working out all things in my life for my good. I will make it through the process because of His love. Father, bring back the dreams and hopes of Your promises to me. Let not my future be robbed anymore by fear or doubt or complaining. Father, don't ever let me judge my tomorrows or even my todays by the trials or failures of my yesterdays. I completely put my trust in

You. Renew my faith to believe You at Your Word that I might obtain the promise that You intended for me. In Jesus' Name, I receive fresh revelation of God's Word and promises. I will be like unto Apostle Paul who said in II Corinthians 12:1 **"It is not expedient for me doubtless to glory. I will come to visions and revelations of the Lord."** *Father, I do not boast in my plea, but I desire all that You have for me. Show me Your Glory and Revelation that I may see clearly."*

CHAPTER FIVE

Desert Bloom or Desert Gloom

Oh the rush that the children of Israel felt! Oh the jubilee and the celebration that went on that glorious day!! Now think about it: Deep dark Slavery for over four-hundred years, their families, their parents, their grandparents, many generations before them suffered at the hand of the Egyptians. Day after day, they were beaten and abused. Children were being raped and killed, all were as sheep led to the slaughter. Not a very pretty picture but it's true and I'm sure it was even worst. We don't even know the half of it. But here it is, the big day that they have hoped for, dreamed about; freedom. Could it be true? Is it real? Tell me one more time, Moses, are we really free. It seems an impossible thought that could only be a dream. It seems it could probably never happen. Really, it is just like you and I were before salvation. Only problem was, most of us did not really know we were in that much trouble. Your world was beaten everyday, abused to whatever your master satan wanted. When salvation, came oh what a release, oh what joy, it could not be explained by the use of just words. I can just hear them as they yelled, **"We are Free! We're free!"** Free was a word not to be used by a slave. I'm sure they laughed with new laughter, sang a new song in their heart, jumped for joy and shouted with ecstasy at the top of their lungs because they, which were bound into deep slavery, were now totally free. Just listen in your minds for a moment to the sound of freedom. What does that sound like to you? I am trying to get you to paint a picture of the joyous sound of that day in your mind. Bells ringing, people crying for joy as hopes are being restored to them as a nation.

I can just picture that day as if it happened in today's world. It would be on CNN: "Yes ladies and gentlemen, the treaty between the great nation of Egypt and the nation of Israel has finally been signed by Pharaoh and his officials. The Israelites are *free*, yes, I did say "*free*". After four hundred years of slavery, this struggle has finally come to an end! Well, Ed, what was the final blow that caused the end of this long reign over these people?"

"Well, Mike, they tell me it's like a miracle but standing live at the Nile River is our man, Jesse, to tell us first hand what's going on. Now don't forget that you have heard it here first on CNN. Now to Jesse."

"Mike I'm here today talking with Joshua, a man that has been a witness to these strange events. So, Joshua when did you first see signs that the table was beginning to turn?"

"Well Jesse, I really thought when we showed up with the snake rod that it was going to do the trick, you know, it kind of scared me. But boy, was I surprised when old Pharaoh's priests pulled out a couple of snake rods themselves, real eerie, you know what I mean. But then it got worse and Pharaoh told us to make bricks without straw. About that time I and many of the others were going to go ahead and run Moses right on back to the desert that he came from."

Jesse said, "Well Josh, you don't mind if I call you Josh, right. What kept the fire burning for you to stay with Moses?"

"Hey, making brick without straw might be rough but thinking about being in slavery another four hundred years, you go ahead and figure, what's the choice? Moses was the only hope we had in a long time," replies Josh.

"So you stayed with your man," replied Jesse.

"At first it seems we had to endure a lot more trouble from Pharaoh, as well as the hand of our God. The harder Moses would try, the harder Pharaoh's priest would try. The battle went on, it seemed. One day we had flies in our soup, next day locusts on our bed. If affected our cattle, our water, our homes, everything. But then things got better. It started raining down fire and darkness on Egypt but not on us and all of a sudden, Egypt started treating us with great respect. They started acting as if they were the slaves and we were the free people. They gave us gold and silver and their good things."

"And what did Pharaoh say about all this,

watching his people begin to humble themselves to slaves?" asked Jesse.

"He didn't like it one bit. I think that was the straw that broke the camels back. He got really mad and told Moses just like his father did; he was going to kill our first-born by the morning. We were scared and shaken. Who wants their children killed, a price too high for even our freedom? But boy wasn't Pharaoh surprised when he woke up the next day and it was his own firstborn that was killed. About that time, it was a sad moment for all of us, but you know, Pharaoh relinquished his hold on us and let us go. Praise be to God," said Josh.

"Well there you have it, reporting live from the Nile River, where you hear news first, back to you Ed..."

Now you can see that was a powerful day, a day where the greatest power on earth was humbled and destroyed by the God of their slaves. Awesome wasn't it? That day has affected mankind forever. You know when you think of it, it was the same thing that our Lord Jesus Christ has done for us. At that time, we served the god of slaves. Yes, we were slaves to sin and the devil, whether by choice or unknowingly, that is what we were. He sent His Deliverer, His only son Jesus Christ, to come to earth and set His people free. By redemption of His Son we have been delivered. At that statement is where you, the reader is supposed to go buck wild into praise for your Lord, the living King. Do I hear "AMEN!"?

What an incredible story and what a mighty celebration. Let's not forget this as we go on into this chapter of the book. I still can hear the music and celebration of the newfound freedom ringing in the air. We're free, we're free, and we're free!!!! This is what they were thinking: "We did it, and we finally made it. All of our sorrows are gone. Goodbye ole task master, goodbye lashing of the whip, good riddance ye ole brick pit and we're out of here." I'm sure at this time they thought, "All my troubles are gone far away; we are going to the Promised Land." They were uncertain of exactly where they were going, but they just went in hope of a better place. I guess they figured any place had to be better than Egypt. So off they went, rejoicing blindly into the desert, carrying with them all of their belongings. The first few days were just amazing to them, no master to serve; no Egyptians to bow to or to wait on. They were able to just take care of themselves and their family. Freedom at last but at what price. That was what they had to think about.

Kind of like us when we get saved, oh what a celebration to be born again into His marvelous light, never to be the same. We declare we are free. We jump and shout about it but do we have an understanding of the price that is about to come to get us to our promised land that the Lord has promised us. Are we like the children of Israel, not careful to think of what's ahead, just blindly going out to the wilderness, so we can get to our promise land? It has been paid for already, many may say on their way. Didn't Jesus deliver us from the bondage that we were in, so we could easily just get there? I guess that's what the children of Israel thought, "We will just get there. Let's celebrate." Now don't get me wrong, I believe that the price has been paid and I'm right along side of you jumping and celebrating the victory that we have in Jesus. Just like Moses and his people when they were delivered, they just went for it and said, "Off to the desert we go." Lord wherever you lead me I'll go, kind of like when you got saved. If you were like me you said, "*Jesus, I'll follow you all the way, wherever you would go.*" Barely and most likely, we have not given any thought to what that might have really meant. We are just going! Take me to the desert, the land of snakes and scorpions where there is no food to eat, and hardly no water to be found. Oh yea don't forget, there were enemies all around but hurried off they went. Don't get me wrong I'm sure they were not thinking that, but it was still true. It could be the promise land or the Kingdom of God, or maybe some great goal in your life that you are trying to get to. In the beginning the idea of that goal seems so great, freedom from the old way of life to a greater life. But I promise, it is off to the desert you go. It seems no matter what you are aiming for, that desert experience is going to show itself up sooner or later and in most cases, it is sooner. You may be finding yourself planning on a new career or maybe it's a wife or husband. You might have great plans for the ministry or some great thing you want to accomplish in life. Don't think I want to take that from you. I don't. Go ahead and rejoice now as you begin to go on your way. Shout with a great shout of victory.

Salvation is great, goals and plans are great and they may all be delivered to you by our great and awesome God. But they come with a price; it's not easy and it's never free. Just as the children of Israel embarked on their way out to the promised land, so must we in our lives. But it is this desert experience that will tell the story for us.

Now let's look back at the children of Israel. Well, they gathered their things and left, wiped the dust off of their feet and they were not looking back. They did not have to be told twice. So out to the wild blue, hopeful yonder they went with God on their side and a goal in their heart, friends and family rallying around them. They were going to possess their promise land.

If the story would stop here it would be a glorious story of how people with a vision would have obtained their freedom, all glory to God. But we know that it did not stop there. They still had to obtain the promise by following their unseen God through the desert and that would make it self-real to them in the days ahead.

"Desert bloom or desert gloom," that is what the next few chapters in the book of Exodus would reveal to us. For most of Israel it was desert gloom. Only two of the original families made it into the Promised Land, Joshua and Kaleb; not too encouraging that only two made it. Well, I have got good news; it does not have to be that way with you or me. We can make it in. Oh there is still a desert to go through but we have a way maker that can make a way where there seems no way. I know what you are saying, "What do you mean they had God Almighty Himself manifesting on the scene and they did not make it? What chance do you think we have?" You have more than just a chance, have you ever heard hindsight is 20/20. Well, here is your chance to put understanding to your knowledge. You and I can take what we have learned from Moses and the children of Israel and put that knowledge to work for us. Let's look at what they did with God's Word and provision and compare that to what we are doing. Let's see if we are living as they did at first or if we are taking God's Word as just mere words on a page. Are they Words to be easily forgotten at the first sign of trouble or despair or are they Words that are everlasting to everlasting? Trust me, His Word is true and everlasting.

Now the victory has been won! Oh how they would tell their children's children of this battle and all of what their great God has done for them. What an awesome day! But it was not long into the desert (on their pathway to the promise) that the sun began to beat on their heads. Their heart began to faint as they wandered in the desert. Some saying, "Did we not say, leave us in Egypt where we had food and drink." Others were saying, "Were there not enough graves in Egypt that you brought us out here to die?" Now think about it, these were the same people who just saw the greatest power in earth. They watched the ones who had held them captive for over four hundred years bow their will, their strength and power to the Hebrew God and let them go. Oh what a celebration! You remember we just read about the victory, the celebration of freedom. But now with a little heat on, they want to curse Moses and go home. Is that not like ourselves too many times? We make great plans, we believe God is with us, and we even see His hand setting things in motion but when the heat gets on, our tongues and evil hearts begin to wag like a dog's tail. Blah, blah, blah.

You say, "I don't have an evil heart." Well before you let yourself get off the hook, remember Peter. He was a mighty man of God who was just trying to help. In Matthew 16:23 (N.I.V) ***"Jesus turned and said to Peter, Get behind me Satan! You are a stumbling block to me. You do not have in mind the things of God, but the things of man."*** What a key verse. No, I'm not saying you are an evil person. But I am saying anything that is against the Word or Will of God is not right and that's what we do when we whine and complain. In that verse Jesus said some simple but powerful words. He told Peter, "You do not have in mind the things of God, but the things of man." So many times we don't make it through because our mindset is earthly, worldly, and fleshy instead of the mind of Christ. You see the Israelites already forgot their great hope of freedom, the notion to be their own nation under God, their thought of what God did to the Egyptians and all their hope of where they were going. Soon it passed from there as they began to take on the mind of man instead of the mind of God and they whined and complained, forgetting the road they were on would lead them to their promise. So please even though the road around you may be hard and hot and filled with sweat running down your brow, don't give in. You may have enemies on every side. Your load and burdens may ever be too heavy for you, but don't forget the road you are on is the one to your promise. The Israelites had a cloud by day and a fire by night that would go before them where the presence of God did dwell. It was leading them through to where they needed to go, but a little lack of water, or food, too much sunshine and heat, and off they go forgetting the truth.

Don't forget that you are on the road to your promise. It doesn't matter how hard the road is, it does not matter how hot it gets. It does not matter that the enemies are on every side and the road you've taken seems too long and you know that there is a short cut down there, and an easier way over here. You might even know other people who cross their desert this other way. Don't despise the way of the Lord or how His hand leads you. The road you are on is for you. It was not for God. He took the Israelites the long way and it was for the Israelites, so he could prove them, show up mighty for them and sift their hearts that when they would get to the promised land and obtain their promise, they would have been a vessel worthy of the prize. So your way may seem hot and hard, long and dry and your friends may not have to go that way. Your family before you, they did not have to go that way, but

I'm telling you they are not reaping the harvest of the promise land like you are. The children of Israel years before had then never tasted freedom, never saw their own sunshine, never ruled their own lives, never felt the freedom of leaving Egypt to go to a better land. But a price must be paid to get to that promise, like a sweet box of alabaster, there is a high price to be paid. So is it with the promise of God, yes, given so freely. But on the way the cost is high, but oh, the prize of reaching that goal. It's where you have never gone, a place that you have never obtained before. It's there. It's on the other side of this scorpion and viper-filled land where the water is dry and the sun is hot. Even if there are a million people around you, it's still lonely and hard. Just don't be like Peter or the children of Israel were at the moment when they took on the mind of man and not of God. They forgot that they were on the road to a promise. Be of good cheer, my friend, your life might be like a big long desert but I've got hope for you. It's your road to the promise. How awesome is God? He is so Awesome! Hallelujah, I've just got to praise Him.

Trails and deserts, all of the hard efforts, whatever it takes to get to the promise, it's worth it. You can do the impossible. Don't stop dreaming of what God has for you and don't let go. You may say, "What I want seems impossible. It's way out of my reach." I'm telling you, for over four hundred years the children of Israel dreamed the impossible dream and one morning, their children woke up free. For years man dreamed of flying and one day the Wright

Brothers took their first flight. You say oh, but they were great people. No, they were as simple and normal as you and I. But they added hope and faith to their dreams and believed through all of the failures and heartaches, through all the let-downs and disappointments. Though it was all they could see, the goal and the promise would be reached. Through the rainy day, even though it is pouring down upon you, don't give up. See through the rain. It shall pass, see through the pain, it shall pass. See through all the "I cant's", it will pass. But it is up to you, will you allow God to fulfill His Word to you? Take on His mind, think like He thinks. Believe like He believes and charge with victorious celebration. The hell you are going through is your road to the promise. It reminds me of an old song, " I can see clearly now the rain is gone. I can see all the obstacles in my way. It's going to be a bright, bright sunshiny day." Well that song is for you and me and anyone else who is in the desert of desire on their way to the promise. Don't look at the rain but see past to His Word, His promise, His Hope, His joy. He wants to do good for you. He says in Jeremiah 29:11 " *I know the plans I have for you declares the Lord . Plans to prosper you and not to harm you, plans to give you hope and a future.*" God almighty loves you and desires for you to make it through. Don't look to be delivered from, or taken out of the process. That means you might have to go through it again. Look to make it through because on the other side is your promise of victory.

Now let's look back at the children of Israel. So the children of Israel went on into the desert, still not glorying in their road to paradise, fearful and wanting, even after the Red Sea. They finally watched as those soldiers who beat them and cursed them died. They were swallowed up by the ocean before their very eyes. Oh, it brought on a great celebration, indeed, as it should. Just like us when we get a great victory, we celebrate it. Some monument it, others roll with it and then some ignore it. It is true we can't live on yesterday's victories, but we sure can learn from them and grow from them. It did not take long for them to begin to whine and cry more, always seeming to disobey the Lord. Moses left them for forty days to go up to the mountain of God to get His Word and by the time He got back, they were fornicating, being riotous, building themselves a god of the world made of gold, offering sacrifices, taking on idols and more. I know as we read this we'll think that we would never do such a thing. Well Moses was the voice of God to the people, he was like unto the presence of God to man. Just think when our hard times come and the voice of God seems silent. No one can be found. What do we do? Oh no, I'm sure we're not fornicating but are we searching in other places, finding ourselves in the land of doubt and unbelief, maybe even building up our own security in something tangible that we can trust in. It's all the same. I'm not throwing condemnation at you, instead I'm saying, "Be strong in the Lord, and in the power of His might." "When the going gets tough, the tough get going," I'm sure you've heard. That's kind of what the children of Israel did and we seem to do a lot. The Egyptians could have crushed them under their chariot wheels and their army would have destroyed Israel.

At the Red Sea, the Lord told Moses, **"The**

Lord will fight for you; you need only to be still." (Exodus14:14 NIV) Awesome words. Just be still. He does not need any help. You don't have to make any golden image to lead the way and you don't have to gather the people together to fight your battle. You don't have to put your trust anywhere but in Him for He cares for you and He will fight for you so the next time the going gets tough, let the tough get still. Be still before your God and watch the Lord arise to His battle plan where no devil in Hell can stand. No problem can overcome you. No enemy can lie in wait to steal and kill for truly the battle is not yours, it is the Lord's.

If Israel would have only gotten that truth into their heart along the way. Oh, what more victories would have been won. Well you and I, we can call upon the one who hears and answers prayers, desert or not. Read Psalms 96-98, it's good stuff. Psalms 99:6-9 ***declares that the Lord answers prayer to them that call upon Him.*** Even now in the desert of your situation, there will be opportunity to turn back, to look back from where you left to get to where you are going. I'm sure it might have been easier just staying on the shore, not going out to the deep. You might even have forgotten the promised land, the goal to where you were going in the first place. Maybe you've made a few pit stops and you're kind of stuck right there along the way. Well just let Him pick you up and breathe fresh air to your vision, a new hope. Dream it for the first time all over again. You can make it with and by Christ Jesus your helper. You will paint the colors of your dreams all over again. Name that goal, see it in your mind, don't let go. I promise, just as it was for the children of Israel, the promise was on the other side of the desert, so is it for you. Maybe it's not in plain sight, but it is there. The Word says that He that endures to the end shall be saved. Hold on, this is true. He who gets to the other side shall obtain the promise. Some of you have had promises, hopes and dreams that have gone by, long gone, forgotten. You've received them with joy, gladly planned and hoped for them, but the desert of life has washed some of them away. The sandy storms have beat at them way too long and the illusions and mirages of the prize faded away. Don't give up! He will resurrect all that He promises. The Israelites did not know where they were going or how they were going to get there, they were just glad to go. A hope and a promise of a better place was soon forgotten in their pain. Look at the road you are and make sure God is leading you by His Holy Spirit. Don't lose sight of Him, go deep into the desert of desire all the way to your promised land for it is the road to your promise.

The path is not always easy but you will become (if you let Him) the vessel of honor, worthy of the prize. You will be like a prize fighter after he trains and trains, then he must fight to the end to get to the desired goal. For when he wins, the victory is great. So keep your eyes on the goal, not the desert surrounding you. They will lie to you, but He, Christ Jesus, will give you truth. 1 Corinthians 9:24 ... *"Run in a way that you shall receive the prize,"* and Philippians 3:14 says *"Press on toward*

the goal to win the prize for which God has called." Don't let go of that! It is God who has called you out from bondage into freedom of the desert, to reach the other side of the promise. There is where you will bloom in Him and obtain your victory. **Always remember that you are a son or daughter of the Most High God.**

CHAPTER SIX

The Heart of Despair

Oh the pain of despair, there is nothing like it. Do you ever feel like the Word of the Lord is only **mere words on a page**, allowing despair to settle in on your situation? After hope is gone, doubt floods in, and it seems no relief is in sight, it's then we come to despair. The result is a heavy heart, a heart that is so weighed down that it can't truly believe the Word of the Lord anymore. It is a heart that begins to compromise with the Word of the Lord. It thinks that the Word is not true or maybe you think you can help the Word of the Lord. Maybe you don't say any of these things, but your actions begin to speak them loud and clear. You might just give up on the Word of the Lord that is in your heart. The heart of despair is the perfect ground for compromise to begin to arise in your life. Compromise is the biggest tool to get you right out of the will of the Father. It gets you from doubt to despair, hopelessness to destruction. Then you will lose all of the power needed to see it through and to accomplish the plan of the Lord. All of this is caused by the loss of hope, the settling in of doubt that gets overtaken by despair until it leads you down to the path of destruction. Finally, you lose the battle.

If only we could see 98% of the battle is won

or lost by what's in our mind and heart. This is why you cannot give in to the heart of despair, doubt, unbelief, blame, confusion, hopelessness, fears or uncertainty. These are all the ingredients that you need to cause the Word of the Lord to become just mere words on a page instead of the all-powerful truth. I know it's not easy and sometimes reality seems bigger than what you know in your heart to be true but you must be steadfast, holding on and declaring the truth. As a man speaketh out of his heart, so is he. What are you speaking? What are you believing? What are you declaring over your life and the life of others? Is it the fact of reality or the truth of the Word? Despair comes to kill and destroy all that which has come to bring life so shake yourself or do whatever you have to do to get rid of it. Jesus went to raise a little child from the dead, and because of despair and doubt in those around Him, He cast out everyone from where He was; and then He was able to raise the child. So you see how powerful doubt and despair are; they are killers, robbers, hope-stealers and life- destroyers. Even the master of Heaven and Earth could not work in their presence. So He did what He knew to do, cast it out, far away from Him. You should do the same thing. Cast it off of you so that you may be able to obtain all of what God has for you.

The answer to all that you have need of is sometimes right behind the door of despair. Don't get me wrong, I'm not saying you should be in despair (God forbid) but if you are there, cast it off and walk through the door of faith and truth and God's unfailing love for you. The whole key of despair is to get you to believe something other than the Word of the Lord. Our awesome loving God gave Himself for you and this world, came from Glory, took the penalty of sin, died, and then rose again. After the resurrection, He sent us His Holy Spirit. Then the Word said that ***Jesus is ever making intercession for us at the throne room of Heaven***. But you might feel like He doesn't love us enough to answer us or help us out of this mess we got ourselves in, I say **"No"**. He is an awesome loving God who delights to do His children good and not harm. He will come to your aid, yes, He will come to your rescue and forgive you or heal you. He will provide all that you have need of if you only believe to the end. Somewhere along the way, He will manifest His Glory until the fulfillment of His Word. This is the promise of God to you.

You see, you never have to be in despair. Sure it hurts and sometimes gets very hard along the way, but consider our God is faithful. Just for this moment, consider God the Father who is in love with you, faithful and true, then the clouds of despair will begin to split apart as the Red Sea did for the children of Israel. And as the waters of despair begin to part, then the Glory of God can come and carry you over to the other side. You will walk on dry land on the way to your promised land and the enemy of despair will get swallowed up in waters and winds of His Glory. ***Remember Jesus loves you and desires for all of your needs to be met***. He has a purpose for you, to bless you and lead you into His plan. It's a good plan to prosper you and bring you health, joy and wealth to fulfill the very desire of your life. So, if it is easy to give up on God's Word and release ourselves to doubt and fear, let's make it just as easy to give up on fear and doubt and release ourselves to God's Word of faith, hope, and love. For by faith, the righteous have obtained a good report before the Lord. From this day on, we will walk in the faith that He (*being God*) will complete and finish His awesome work in us. For He loves me right now as I am. *To God be the Glory!*

CHAPTER SEVEN

Is There Not a Cause?

Mere words on a page, that's what it seems like sometimes to me. The mountains won't move, the pain won't leave, money always finds itself somewhere else or in somebody else's pocket. When will what I believe be true? What about the promise of God to me? Those are our thoughts sometimes or am I the only one that feels like some of my dreams or hopes may never come true. If you are honest with yourself, you can go ahead and admit it. There is no one else here, just me and you. Let me help you, begin to fight back now. You know the old saying, "Never pin a pig up in a corner, he'll come out fighting." Well, that was David's plan.

Let's look back on David as he was just a little boy. "Is there not a cause, is there not a cause?" That is what David yelled out to the men that came from the battle as the cowardly yielded themselves behind the rocks as not to be seen by the giant. Oh what a prize that they would have received. Oh what great reward and honor from the King they would have gotten, all their troubles would be over, they would be rich. Moving into the King's family and receiving all the rights that come with that would have been their reward. They could have had up to half of the Kingdom if only they would go over there and kill that giant. The very reason they joined the army of the king was to protect their country and provide a safe place for their kingdom to live. Maybe along the way they could move up the ladder, advance in the ranks, gain some respect or fortune or fame, or just a good livelihood. But at this time they had forgotten all of that. Reasons they became who they had become, just then, they couldn't figure out. All their hopes and dreams were before them. They just had one problem, the giant, who in turn wanted to cut their head off and feed it to the birds. That's a big problem wouldn't you say.

Kind of like us, we get a vision or a plan toward a goal or we are trying to accomplish something in our life or maybe it's as simple as believing the Word of God but when it costs more than what we are willing to pay we want to give up. If the circumstances around us raise the heat or if things just don't work out like we wish they would, are we not like the men of the king's army? Are we not backing up, maybe hiding, or hoping someone else will take care of it? Do you just forget the reason you got in the fight in the first place? But no one told me it was going to be this hard. No one said there would be giants so big. So we lose sight of the prize or victory not realizing, that this hard time, this gigantic obstacle in your way is your pathway to victory. It's right through here! Let's not forget that. Overlook your problems and situations, right now for this moment and see your Father and see the prize

He has for you. See the promise of God that you have had to hold on to all of this time and fight like you never have before. Be like David and declare to your spirit, "Is there not a cause? Isn't victory worth it? Isn't the prize worth it? Isn't faith in the Word of God worth it?" What can separate you from the love of God? Will death or life or principalities now or to come? Will bad days or sad days stop you from receiving your promise?

Go out there and kick Goliath in the butt and take that which is yours! *Do not forget the prize*, the reason you started this race. Keep your eyes on the prize, Christ Jesus, the kingdom, the promise that God has given you. Well ask yourself this question. Is there not a cause? Is not the cause better than the obstacles? For the children of Israel it was not, they could not see beyond the desert and the journey. So there in the desert they died. But David, he took the cause to the giant and slew that old problem. That's all it was, a big obstacle, something that stood between him and his goal or promise. Go ahead and be like David, don't be like the cowardly soldiers who began the war with battle and victory in mind. **For there is no victory unless there is a battle.** They forgot the spoil and sweet savor of victory in the sight of this giant so they considered the problem instead of the victory of reward and did not gain either one. They did not fight, so there was no freedom.

Even leaving those problems alone doesn't

solve it for they were in bondage to the Philistines already, the moment they did not go out to battle, they were in bondage. So, just looking at our problem or situation that is in our way is not enough. It isn't until we bring the battle through it. They did not reap the prize of having the victory because without a war there is no spoil to take, no prize to receive, no honor to wear. But we can have a better testimony than this when we set it in our heart that there is a cause. I see victory on the other side. Watch out problem, situation, obstacle, or whatever is standing in your way of receiving the victory in God's plan for you. Start reaping all of the benefits of the Kingdom that He has for you. Go ahead and open a can of whoop-butt on it. Don't quit until you win and receive the prize of the goal and do whatever it takes to get it. Ask yourself, **"Is there not a cause?"** Do you like where you are at, even if you're not in the battle. Do you like running away from the source of the problem or obstacle? The answer I'm sure is, "No." So charge all the way and take that which is yours in Christ Jesus.

Let's, for the moment, bring ourselves to the battlefield of life. Put yourself in a vast valley. (That may seem easy to do, you may already feel as if you're in a valley of despair.) Look around you. Do you see it, that big ugly giant in your way? Place him right in the middle of your pathway of getting to where you're going. You may think that your problem is not exactly in the middle of your way or that it is not always right in front of you. I am here to tell you, let me unveil the lie for you. The enemy (problem) is around you. Maybe it only comes out at night or day, or at work or play, or in your health or your wealth, or whatever it is and whatever it does, that enemy (problem) is right, flat out in the middle of your goal for life and your pathway is blocked.

No, do not learn to live with this enemy! Oh this only comes up now and then. It is since I lost my job or maybe, I'm just not getting what I need at church. Or I'm not getting what I need from my spouse, or I can't sleep, or this one offended me or that one won't stop talking about me, or I hate the way I am. Or maybe you hate how people treat you. Maybe your family has hurt you, or you don't have a good father or good mother or maybe everyone else married the right person except you. Others just seem to be so blessed and you can't get out of the starting line. Maybe it's your boss that quit appreciating you or the church you help never honors you. By now you may say, "Apostle Craig, you are going on and on." This may be true but I want to uncover some hidden giants that we live with. Sometimes we live with them day in and day out under the excuse of "That's life." That is just the way it is supposed to be.

In so many ways in our life, we become like the army of the children of Israel. We see the giant out in the valley, and we go hide behind some rocks hoping he does not see us. We're just looking at it, watching our problem as if it doesn't exist. We're thinking, "I'll leave you alone if you'll leave me alone. I won't bother you if you don't bother me." All the time we're not realizing that the hidden cords of the problem are wrapped around us choking the very life out of us. In most cases, it's like a snake that wraps itself around the victim and then slowly squeezes until its victim has no life in him anymore. So you can be like the children of Israel just standing by the sidelines thinking everything is okay, that you're safe and hidden or you can fight. What they did not realize was that until someone (like yourself) beat the giant in their way, they were already in bondage. Their life had already ended in the way they knew it to be. But the pain of the battle to them was worse than the pain of cowering down before their giant. Is this not like us? From time to time the pain of fighting our fears or problems is greater than the pain of hiding out away from it. Did you not know that at that point, you were already in bondage?

It's time to realize that there is a cause for freedom. It's not to fight with man's hands or to rage some battle on our own. *"Not by might, not by power, but by My Spirit says the Lord of Host."* (Zech 46:15) We must recognize our enemy. It's not your boss, husband or wife, friend or foe, family or financial problems, the flesh and the devil are the real enemies. As the Word says, *"Your battle is not carnal, but mighty through God to the pulling down of strongholds, casting down arguments and every High thing that exalts itself against the knowledge of God, and bring every thought (or emotion) into captivity to the obedience of Christ Jesus." (2 Cor. 10:4-5)* Our enemy always lies in the spiritual work of the devil. To kill a tree, you cannot just cut off its fruit, being the place where it is manifested, and you can't just break the branch, it will grow back. Not even chopping down the whole tree will completely do it. You must get deeper than that, you must go to the root. It is the Devil and his principalities at work in your life that are around you, doing all they can do to snuff the life out of you or to keep you hidden in a corner. I say, **"Attack at the root."** You have all the power and authority to combat this enemy and WIN because you have the author and finisher of your faith, Jesus Christ on your side. I know what you're saying, "It just can't be the devil or evil principalities, it's my husband Joe, or my boss John or maybe, Mike's wife Suzy, or my child Frank, or the banker, or the lack of money in my life, or this sickness." Well I say, "no." Those and all the other problems and situations you can think of and blame it on are not the root. You might even think some of the problem is yourself and decisions you have made. This is all an illusion by the enemy, a smoke screen. So you don't see him, he is hiding in the delusion of your situation. It may be true that you and others may have contributed into this problem but the problem is only the fruit of the tree, it is not the tree. The root is the enemy, the devil. Jesus said in John 10:10 **"The thief does not come except to steal and kill and to destroy, but I have come that they may have life and that they may have it more abundantly."**

Now let's use these guidelines. Become a doctor by the spirit and x-ray your problem. Does it steal from you, does it destroy you, and is it killing parts of your life, or does it bring life with joy abundantly?

All of your symptoms, though they may seem to come from a problem, a bad situation, or childhood abuse are not the real problem. Well, I hate to break it to you but those things can only be dealt with temporarily. Cut it off and sooner or later it will grow back, maybe in a different form, shape or size but eventually, it will come back. So we recognize the spirit behind it and begin to war on that behalf, to win the victory over it. The children of Israel they could have gone and killed some of the Philistines. They could have even captured some, made some as slaves, overpowered some, or even ruled over some. But until they got to the foot, the champion giant, they still would have not received the victory of their enemy. The giant stood there day in and day out, defiant of them, their goals, their life, their plans, their future, and even their God. Until one would recognize hiding from the problem, living on the sideline, hoping it will pass or go away was not their answer. Learning to live with their giants was no better. This only enslaved them, so you must look at yourself and say, "Is there not a cause?" Yes, there is! So I will fight in faith with my God, against my enemy. And with a mouth full of praise, I will dance before Him because I have the victory.

A quick note, this plight was also another's plight in the New Testament. Jesus tells us about some lepers who were outside the camp hiding and starving. They were near death and it was unlawful to go into the city to get food if you were a leper. But they gathered themselves together and said, "Why stay we here, lest we die? For if we go into the city for food, we may be stoned to death but out here we are sure to die." Is there not a cause? So they went into the city and obtained food for their substance and lived. I declare to you, that if you will put away your shame and pride and trust yourselves into the hand of your God, you will take the victory. Stare your enemy in the face and take back what is yours.

Let's look deeper into this. It's not always the devil!!! But the devil is the root of the problem. I do not want to overlook the basic form of the problem. The giant is not just a flesh problem but a spiritual problem. It's not to be mistaken or to be thought of as just a carnal problem. This can not be solved only by the flesh, but by the Spirit of the Lord.

The giants in our life must be and can be destroyed by prayer in the Holy Ghost and a life full of reading the Word of God. With faith and belief that He will do exactly what He said He will do, Father God is waiting for you to begin to take that which is yours. Don't let anything stand in your way. I am sure that David was wondering what happened to the armies of the children of Israel when he got there. I could just see him standing there in front of this army and looking at their fear. And on the other side, he could see the giant, just laughing at this little army that did not know what to do. David said to himself, "Is there not a cause!! What are you doing just standing here, when the battle is right in front of you?" You see, for some reason, they were not prepared for this battle. It was bigger than them, they thought. David, on the other hand, killed a bear when he was out in the field and he also killed a lion so now David was equipped to go out there and kill this giant. He was proven in his faith. That's what I'm talking about. You must be proven in your faith if you're going kill the giants in the land that are attacking you. Let's equip you a little right now. First things first. Everything is not the devil nor is everything spiritual, but it is a spiritual warfare that you are in. The only way to win the fight is a spiritual confrontation that only you can begin.

Right now where you are at, you and only you can do this. Do this by praying continually in the spirit. You must fight because the battle has already begun. Your adversary the devil has already launched an attack against you. So what are you going to do? Will you prepare yourself or will you be like the children of Israel, fearfully hiding behind the rocks? Will you be the one to take the battle to him?

Don't look at your circumstances, or your problems, or at the natural armor, but look unto God, the author and the finisher of your faith. Where is your God, Yahweh, God the Father, the Most High? Is He alive in you or is He dead in you?

It all begins with your faith system, your belief in the Lord. "Neither by might nor by power but by My spirit," said the Lord. Is this what you believe? Is this your truth? Is this your hold? Will you go out and fight the battle, take off your armor of the flesh and put on your armor of the spirit, and begin to rage war in the Heavenlies by the Spirit of the Lord? The only way to possess the new land is to go to new ground (spiritually) that you do not hold just yet. Take it from the enemy of your soul in Christ Jesus. Well you say, don't just try to blame everything on the devil and I'm not. I'm not trying to give you excuses for the mistakes and problems that you may have brought into your life either. But I do want us to look at the root of the problem, there is a force that we seem to overlook so many times in our life working against us. He is called "the devil." You say, "I thought this chapter was, "Is There Not a Cause?" It seems as if it is beginning to sound like 'The Power of the Devil'." Well, nooooooo! But I am not trying to give power to him or show how big he is, or even try to put the blame on him for all the problems in our life. In all actuality I don't want us to overlook the obvious. There is an enemy out there seeking whom he may devour and he may be disguised as a problem, the neighbor next door, or a situation in your life that is killing the life out of you. I am not going to stand for it anymore and I don't want you to stand for it, either. WHY? Why must you just sit there until you are dead? Why can't you receive your healing? Why can't the promise of God be true in your life? Forget past generations, past promises and past happenings. Just because Uncle Bill did it this way or Aunt Susan did it another way doesn't mean you have to do it that way. I'm here to tell you by the Word of the Lord that those things don't matter. You have seen your cousin Patsy die and Grandpa Joe never made it, and so on, and so on. So what.

You want Bible! I'll give you Bible-inspired Word of the Lord. All that stuff and all that you have seen to this point does not matter. Why can't you be the generation that enters the Promised Land? Why can't you be the one that cuts off the giant's head? Why not you be the one that makes the walls of Jericho fall down? Why not you? That is the question that is bombarding my mind today, "Why not you?". So I ask you, "Is there not a cause? Is there not a cause for freedom?". "Freedom from what," you say. You have lived so long with that lying devil of a problem that you can not seem to get rid of it. Maybe your giant is different than mine; maybe it is some sin in your life, like sex outside of marriage, stealing from the government on your taxes, lusting after someone at work. Maybe it could be something simple like hating your neighbor or gossiping around your church or work, or some sickness that won't let go. Some people may read this and wish I had not said that. Think of all those poor people with sicknesses that just can't help themselves and get well. How bad are they going to feel? I am saying for them to get that giant out of their life. They have probably prayed, "Father if it be Your will, please heal me." I'm telling you I would rather offend every sick person out there if I can get only one to believe that they can get that giant of sickness out of their life. I would rather that all of them who are sick believe that God is a healer and He does desire to heal them than for them to go through life not being healed. Having a mind-set that believes if it be God's will, He will do it and He will heal them is not right. It will never happen. These same people are thinking that God has not heard them or He doesn't want to heal them. He has a reason that the people are sick and He wants them that way. I say, "Phooey! That is a big fat lie of the devil." Let's look at Jesus. He said, ***"If you see me, you see my Father and the things that I do are not my things but my Father's in Heaven."*** He went around healing all of them. If you are going to die in your sickness (which I hope that none of you do) then at least die jumping and leaping and praising God for the healing for He is a healer. Whether or not you get healed does not change the fact that He is a healer. Go ahead and cut the devil's head off and the power he has over you and believe for your healing, deliverance, money, health, joy, peace, a husband, a child, a wife, whatever you have need of. Believe for it. He is. That is why His name is ***"I am"*** (Yahweh). He said He would give His people His name and He would be their God and they would be His people. That is why in these last days He has given us His name, ***"Yahweh,"*** (the I Am) because He is the ***"I Am".*** Whether or not you ever get what you think you should get, whether or not you get that right job, that certain wealth, all of your health or whatever it is, He is Yahweh to you, the ***"I am that I am."*** Give the old devil a good kick in the butt and believe in spite of yourself or circumstance. Yell louder than the problem. Shout about the goodness of God right now, I feel the anointing. Let's step out of this book just for a moment and get free. Go ahead and give God the glory and proclaim that He is. Be free, be free. Go ahead and receive all that you need right now. If it is health, if it is wealth, if it is love, or maybe freedom from depression, receive it, right now in Jesus' Mighty Name.

I'm telling you I feel the Holy Ghost. If you will take the words of this book and believe them, **you will never be the same**. I know right now by the Holy Ghost somebody is receiving their healing and somebody's marriage is getting healed. Go ahead and receive it right now. You don't have to wait until some church service happens or some famous preacher prays for you. The Word says, **"Where there are two or more, I'll be there."** You and I can agree right now for whatever you need Him to be. Remember He is the **"I am that I am"** and it's yours right now. I would rather believe Him until the end and have that testimony before my Lord than to give up and accept the things that seem as if I can't change them. So go ahead and take back what is yours by the Spirit of the Lord. This battle is spiritual and must be fought in the spirit, not with man's hands. We can take a lesson from the battle of Jericho. Was it by the hand of the army of Israel that the walls came down or was it a spiritual move of the Spirit? It was by their faith in the face of the enemy that they believed God for the impossible. Without weapons of man or the armor of man, the battle was won. They marched around the wall with the praises of God on their lips and defeated their enemy. So let's do it. Fight until the end with the praises of God on your lips and destroy the giant in your life as you begin to believe God for the impossible again. See Him as the **"I Am that I Am"** once again in your life and He will come through. So am I saying we don't have to deal with the problem face to face or we should deny our sickness or pain? God forbid, no. What I am saying is that you can move the hand of God with your faith. Oh, here is an even a better one. Yahweh, Father God, just told me, you can bless heaven with the confession of your faith. Somehow heaven gets stronger with the confession of your faith. There is a scripture that kind of goes like this in the New Testament, that **we have such a cloud of witness watching us.** Think about it, all of heaven is watching and waiting for the sons/daughters of God to arise in their faith and in their hearts as well as in their confession. You can bless and even better, move heaven. Wow, what a thought! If that is all you get from this book, take and run with it. You, just one person, can move and bless heaven. Awesome!! For there is a cause and that cause is that you and all the sons and daughters of the Lord Most High will arise in the Earth and show forth the Glory of their Almighty God in every situation. **Glory be to the Lamb, Christ Jesus, the only One worthy to open the Book of Life**. It is by His Blood Covenant that you and I may glory in Him.

Rev 22:12-14 Behold, I am coming soon, and I shall bring My wages and rewards with Me, to repay and render to each one just what his own actions and his own work merit. I am Alpha and Omega, the First and the Last (the Before all and the End of all). Blessed are they that do His commandments, that they may have right to the tree of life, and may enter through the gates into the city.

Your name is in the Lambs Book of Life.
Need I say more.
All hail King Jesus!

CHAPTER EIGHT

When the Road Gets Too Long

Do you ever feel that the road you are on may be a little longer than what you might have wanted to travel to get to your destination? Remember when you were a child and you were going on a road trip to a vacation spot. What are those famous words that you would always hear you or you siblings ask? **"ARE WE THERE YET?"** I used to wear those words out when we would go on vacation. We would be traveling around the city or state to get to where we were going and it would not be long before I would begin to wear on my parents' patience by saying, "Are we there yet?". It seems like it would echo in their ears the whole way there. "Are we there yet? Are we there yet?" I know sometimes my parents, if they could have, probably would have put me out the car or locked me up in the trunk. They were so tired of hearing, "Are we there yet?"

Well maybe you and I are a little older now and we might not be on a road trip to a vacation spot with our parents but each and every one of us is on a road trip to destiny. Whether we get there or not is really up to us. Now don't get me wrong, I am not discounting the Word of the Lord in your life or God's ability to perform His Word. Remember the book title is **"Mere Words on a Page."** In this book I am trying to teach and show you how to get the awesome words of the Lord off of the pages of the Bible and into your life. I have found out that lots of times it has a lot to do with you and your obedience to position yourself to receive the fulfillment of the Word of the Lord in your life. Furthermore I would like it stated that God (Yahweh) the Most High has no problem accomplishing His Word or making His word come to pass. If there is any reason in the world that a Word of the Lord does not come to pass in your life or the life of another, it is human error. Some have not believed, pursued, positioned, prepared, or done all the other things that it takes to accomplish that word that God gave them or to accomplish what they have read in the Bible. Even with all of our shortcomings, failures and sins, if we repent and move on and call upon Him, He will redeem us. That's what I love about God. Not only will He redeem us from our sins, He can make a way for the Word of the Lord to come to pass in our lives. It might not come in its original form because you have changed the circumstances that God was maybe going to move in your life with. Still, He is more than able to redeem His word to you or give you a new one for you to move toward.

You say, "Apostle Craig, how is this so?" I thought, "God said it, I believe it, and that settles it." Oh how I wish that were true. It would be a wonderful world. If all God had to do was to say something, you and I believe it, and it would come to pass, that would be great. Well as good as it sounds, it takes a little more detail than that to accomplish the Word of the Lord. You say, "No that can't be, He is God. Whatever He says comes to pass. Apostle Craig, are you saying that something can stop the Word of the Lord? If God said it, it might not come to pass? Is that what you are saying?" Well not exactly. Don't forget, I believe that God's Word is above everything and He rules on High and His word as well as His love is from everlasting to everlasting. If I could just stop there, then you and I would easily live in the world of our dreams. God would just have to say it, you and I would believe it and it would be so. Don't get me wrong, I really do believe that statement for myself, but once again I must clarify to you that it is much deeper than that. It takes more to get to the end result. If it weren't so, the whole world would be saved. God Himself said that He wishes none would perish. He also said you should prosper and be in health, so none of us should be sick or poor. We should be healthy as an ox and as rich as a king, able to do all we want to do. You and I both know that this does not always happen. So does that make God's Word untrue? Absolutely not. It just means that it takes a little more than reading a scripture or hearing a word and 'poof, it's there.'

Jesus told Peter, "Come on out of that boat and you can walk on water with me". Now do you and I believe that this was the spoken Word of the Lord? Of course we do, those words Jesus spoke were true to life. But when Peter walked on the water, it did not take long before Peter began to sink. Did this make the Word of the Lord untrue? No! But it shows how we must line up in our lives with King

Jesus in all things to accomplish His Word to us. As always our loving Jesus reached out and caught Peter by the hand and brought him safely to the boat. Even if we fail, His love for us will catch us and see us through. We might have not accomplished the goal of that Word. For Peter it was to walk on water, but he did not make it for long. Still Jesus protected and loved His servant as He loves me and you. With Peter, he only walked on water a few steps. Somehow in that water walking journey, Peter began to fall and Jesus made a way for him. Believe it or not, even with that failure under his belt and many other failures to come, ***Apostle Peter was one of Christ's greatest disciples. So shall you be....***

CHAPTER NINE

THE WORD OF GOD- IS IT REAL TODAY TO YOU?

"Of course," you will probably cry out. **What a question!** What does the writer mean, "The Word of God, Is It Real Today?" Well I find myself reading the Word (**Holy Bible**) and listening to what the different writers are saying, wondering how God did this and how God did that awesome thing. How did this one become a great conqueror over his enemies by His God, and how did this one become a great leader, or how did another one become wealthy or well known, and I can go on and on. God showed up in so many people's lives in the Bible. It seems as if God's Word was endless and always showing up. Just read II Samuel 22 and Psalms 18-21 and you will hear King David declare the greatness and awesome power of his God. How mighty King David had become because of His God. God moved so powerfully and creatively for King David, even before he was King. When He was just a little boy in the field, the Lord strengthened David to protect himself against a bear and a lion. On both occasions, God showed up for David and by God's power, David became the victor as he killed the animals. Then as the battle of the Philistines raged against Israel, David was sent to check on his brothers. He was sent to see of this war. When he found his brothers and the army of Israel cowering behind the hills, David shouted, "Is there not a cause?" But the men were afraid and David declared, "Who is this

uncircumcised Philistine that would come against the armies of God?" He would, himself, take care of Goliath. So you know the story. It wasn't before sundown and David had already killed the giant, cut off his head, and scattered the Philistine army by the power of his God.

Look at Moses when God delivered the Israelites with a mighty hand of power; God cut down the most powerful nations and armies in the world with a shepherd and the Word of the Lord. Think of the plagues and curses that came upon Egypt, all by one man's word. Think of how the Red Sea opened up and swallowed all of Moses' enemies. Think of how the plague brought death to the first-borns in Egypt and I could go on and on. God has proven Himself so many times in the Word, from Genesis to Revelation. We see the might and power, wisdom and love of God towards man. But the real question is how can we get it off of the pages of the Bible to us today. Have you ever asked yourself how the stories in the Bible affect our lives today? Why do these things that I read in the Bible seem not to happen today? Where is all that power? Why does it seem only to be for the chosen few, not for all Christians? Well if you are like me, you have asked that question probably more than once in your Christian walk. Most people try to write off questions like that as a lie of the devil or a spirit of doubt and unbelief. In their minds if they doubt or question God, they will get told things like, "That's not God's will" or "God is not doing that today." If you do hear of something supernatural happening, you write it off as fake or come up with some other explanation. It may sometimes seem like an unsolved mystery. How do we get the total Bible, not just parts, but all of it to become more than just mere words on a page? How do we get it to become more than hope that fades away, or a problem that only time can heal? God wants this for us. He is an awesome, unchanging, loving God who is longing and waiting to show up in your life today. Most people will, because of religion, go through their whole life hoping on the Word of God. Heartache after heartache is received along the way. Then they just put up with it because they won't question the Word of God and its reality for today's world. You say, "Apostle Craig, are you telling us to question God's Holy Word and rebel against the Lord Most High." **Of course not**. I don't want you to question God or why His Word is not producing fruit and action in your life. I want you to question yourself. Stop just accepting Christianity and the Bible and the Word of the Lord as a fairy tale that may one day come true. If it is not coming true today and if it's not to its fullest potential, the blame is not really in the Word of the Lord or its author and authority.

The breakdown in its power and authority to move and change your world, your happening and your surrounding is upon your shoulders. Who are we kidding? The reason we put up with most of the stuff that happens to us or comes our way is not because we don't believe that the Word of the Lord is real or that our God is not real. We don't doubt that God is capable of doing anything. We are not questioning to find out the real answer because it is easier to believe false hope: 'Maybe one day', 'Well that's just the way it is', or any other excuse that comes along. Then to probe deeper and find out in most cases, it's not the lack of God's power or His willingness to accomplish the task before Him, but our willingness to do all we are supposed to do to put action to our faith and cause heaven to move. No wonder there are very little moves of the power of God today. We have become a society of fast food, fast cars, fast women, whatever we want. Whatever vain inquisition you can think of, we want it now. We want drive-through religion, three songs, short sermon, and a prayer and offering. Come on, we get mad because the microwave is not fast enough. We have become a popcorn religion that we are all cooking for the powerless church. Something to make us feel good, not changed is what most of us want to hear. If the preacher says something you don't like, you either leave or vote him out. Man has taken the church into his own hands and that's why you have dry bones all over the place that just won't seem to come together. Because the people can tell you more about their favorite movie, their best song, or what's on television but are not sure of the Word to them, the Word of the Lord seems empty. But when it doesn't work for them, they want to blame God. Do you know what happens when you microwave fruit to heat it up? In most cases, you kill all the nutrients from the inside out. It may look like a fruit on the outside, but is has nothing left but empty calories, nothing that can give life. And for the most part, that's what the church world has become, a well packaged, microwaveable church, full of no substance, producing very little fruit that remains and it brings the Word of the Lord to no effect.

The Word of the Lord is like a solid leather sock, by itself it looks good, but it just lies there. But put a foot in that sock and now it walks and kicks and goes places. Well the embodiment of the Word of the Lord is up to you and me. It is up to us to get the awesome, precious Word of the Lord, off of the pages of the Bible, out of our minds and thoughts, and put them into action. You cannot just name it. You cannot just frame it, you can't program it. You must become it; a living breathing son or daughter of the Most High God, full of His power, and glory, and His wisdom and knowledge. Be one pursuing the Lord and winning the battle as the mighty one that the Word declares you are. But you will first have to give up religion and couch potato spiritual mentality. Put on becoming a son or daughter, one who is moved only by the Word of the Lord and the relationship you have with God through Jesus Christ by the working power of the Holy Spirit.

I have asked before and it will be a question that I keep before you. Is the Bible or the Word of the Lord real to you today? The answer is unequivocally, 'yes, without a doubt,' but it can not stand alone. It must have the embodiment of a son or daughter of the Most High God. It can do nothing without you. You know there is an old saying, "Just because you are standing in a garage does not make you a car." Well, that is the same thing with the Word of the Lord. It can sit next to your bed, on the coffee table, or near the toilet, you may even pick it up on a regular basis and read it, but until it becomes you, until the Spirit of the Word of God falls upon your spirit and enters your soul and mind and is mixed with faith, joy, hope and belief, then it is just words on a page. But you, that's right you, you are the key to the very existence of the Word of God. The Father had you in mind way before He ever made the Word of God (the Holy Bible). Remember in Genesis when He walked with man in the cool of the day. That was His real plan, not a book of law, principles, and blessings. He wanted you to carry His promise and His will all the time because you were His child. But man fell and sin entered into the earth. And the fall of man would start a new era of God's relationship with man. But even in that, He loved us and wanted to reveal Himself to us. He put it down in words as He showed up in people's lives. That is the Holy Bible. God still wants to write His book but not just in the pages of the Bible, but in your heart and soul and mind, and in your life that the Glory of God can be revealed in the earth. Allow Him to do this so all may see Him, through His splendor, as He performs those wonderful secret words that are on those pages inside and through you. You now become the express image of God, His Holy Testament, in the earth. WOW, what an awesome plan that even before you were born, He knew you and predestined you to be His glory in the earth and you can and you shall as you get His Word to become more to you than just mere words on a page.

CHAPTER TEN

Jesus Christ, Your Anointed King and Priest

Ephesians 1:22-23 *"And He (being God the Father) put all things under His feet and gave Him (Jesus Christ) to be Head over all things to the church, which is His body, the fullness of Him who fits all in all."* I can't help but get excited and I want you to join me right now in celebration of who Christ Jesus is. Come on and jump right on in. Some of you have not gotten overly excited about who Jesus Christ is since your salvation. You have moved on to bigger and better things, more knowledge or more law. Who knew that the sparkle in your eye may not be Jesus anymore. Just for this one moment, if I can leave you with anything from this book, it is to reignite the flame of the Holy Spirit of love toward the Son Jesus Christ. Even the very whisper of His name drives you into a Holy fury of the revelation of who He is and who He is in you. If you would let me reach down deep in your spirit, right through your soul, and spark the flame of His glory. Jesus, Jesus, Jesus. So awesome! Think about it. God the Father (**Yahweh**) so loved us that He allowed Jesus in all of His glory to leave His duty, His Holy place on the throne and humble Himself to come down to earth as just a natural man. He was born of a virgin, the answer of the promise. He took on the likeness of man and lived a perfect and Holy life before God.

Jesus walked among man and showed the Glory of God on this earth wherever He went. Awesome things happened wherever He went: healing the multitude, raising the dead, calling man unto God. He then became our petition and took our place for sin. Oh, I need to say that one more time. If that doesn't stir your spirit, something is wrong, He being the deity of God, came and took your place for sin. He took your place on that cross (which represents death). You don't have to die now but you can live, yes live, eternally with the Father. If that won't put a little skip in your step today, you need to rethink it. **Glory, Glory, Glory.** Oh I feel like shouting. You may think, 'Over a little thing like that? Oh, I know I'm saved.' Yes, I'm sure you do but does it move you? Are you grateful? He is the petitioner for our sin, He is the breach restorer between you and God. Without Jesus Christ you could and would not have relationship with the Father. It would be impossible. But by His grace, we are born again. And I'm not ashamed of the Gospel of Christ, it is the way of salvation. Yes salvation, the simple but powerful truth of life, Jesus Christ, King of Kings and Lord of Glory. **All power**, I said, **all power has been given to Him on this earth and then given to "you."** Oh, what a great revelation. Shout somebody! Have you lost your shout? Does the mere mention of His name not move you anymore? Have you forgotten how precious salvation is through Jesus Christ, or how much of a price He paid to get it for you? How many of you can or would give your son for this world (a people that always refuted you and goes against everything you say)? We won't even let the guy pass us on the interstate without getting upset, I'm sure we would not give up a child for the lives of a stranger or even a friend. Oh, what a simple truth. But if you let me, I'll stir up this revelation of the power of the seed, being Christ Jesus, that you have in you. So that truth alone will overcome every battle in your life.

Jesus Christ, I love the mention of that name. All devils in this world shake at the power of that name. There is no sickness, no disease, no lack, no poverty, or any other thing that is bigger than the name of Jesus Christ. In this book I'm going to believe that power and truth is in you. **Jesus, Jesus, Jesus or in the original Hebrew "Yeshua". Oh the power of that name and who He is!** I just can't get enough of it. I remember a song I used to sing in church as a little boy; it went, *"Jesus, Jesus, Jesus, there's just something about that name. Master, Savior, Jesus, Let all Heaven and Earth proclaim, Kings and Kingdoms shall all pass away, but there is something about that name."* Simple little words in a song, but there is enough truth in that song to break open the gates of Hell and destroy every principality that comes against you. With the true revelation of the Name and person of Christ Jesus living and abiding in you , you can defeat the enemy. Think about God in the flesh, becoming man, resurrected from the dead, now sitting on the right hand of the Father in all of His deity. Continually the scriptures says *"making intercession for you, and He is living in you, making your heart (spiritually) a dwelling place."* All the power of God in all of His majesty, His Holy, courageous, mighty, supreme being is living in you. I can't think of enough adjectives to describe our Lord and Savior Jesus Christ. Now He resides in you. Try that on for size. Look yourself in the mirror and tell yourself that, tell yourself who you are in the mirror. Don't do this if you're driving, but if you're not, look right into your eyes, the windows of your soul, and proclaim that the King of Kings, Lord of Glory lives in you. Now think about that. That's a lot to swallow if you really believe it. You say, I know Jesus lives in me, I'm a deacon or I'm a singer, or I preach or teach Sunday School or maybe a Bible study or better yet, I've been saved for "thirty years". That's all fine and well, but how big of a difference is knowing that Jesus Christ lives in you, making Him your life.

Let's look at what I mean. Let's imagine the president or some great king was coming to your house for a year, what would you do? Would your house just stay the same? Would you pull out the best dinnerware? Would you use the best silverware? Would you fix up all the broken down items in that house? Wouldn't you clean it spotless, dress your best, speak in your best language, and show forth all the honor you could? And then what about your friends, neighbors, wouldn't they know? They would probably invite themselves over to see if you really had the president or a king at your home. Forget the neighbors you would probably not leave it there, you would have C.N.N. over, telling the world of this great experience. I've said this to say, "Do you think that you have the same zeal for the real King living in your house as you would for an earthly king? Are you bringing out your best for Him? Do you have daily fanfare for the Lord? Are you giving Him all the time due to Him? Are you telling your neighborhood and your world around you of this King? Are you shouting it at the top of your lungs that there is a King in your heart?" Or are you like so many Christians, yea, come on in Lord? I have Jesus Christ in my heart, all excited at first but as years go by, you can read a book like this and the writer can say, "Pull over and look in the mirror and declare Jesus Christ is in your heart," and you first thought is, 'I've done that already. I know that. Or so, I got that already. Give me real meat of the Word.' Well if the TV remote did not have more of your fingerprints than your Bible and your golf game more time than your prayer life and if you didn't spend more money on going out to eat each week than what you give to God, I might believe you. And if you didn't spend most of your time involved in your car and maybe little or no time winning the lost, I would say sure that might have been a true statement. But I'm trying to rekindle the flame of how awesome that statement is . Reminds me of another little song I used to sing in Sunday School "***Love is the flag flown high over the castle of my heart, yes the*** *castle of my heart, over the castle of my heart. Love is the flag flown high over the castle of my heart that the King's in residence here. So wave it high in the sky let the whole world know, let the whole world know, let the whole world know, so wave it high in the sky and let the whole world know that the King is in residence here."* That King, greater than any king or president in this earth, past president or any to come, now resides in you. That's good news. Get that in your spirit; go back to that simple truth. Jesus lives here. Think about it, I wonder if a King lives there how much would that really change your life.

Well it's true, and if you have this revelation it will change you forever. Is the King in residence in you? What flag is flying over your heart? Is it the flag of His kingdom or are you at truce with some other king? Remember Asa in II Chronicles 15-16. As long as he trusted in God and honored God in all of his household, his kingdom was at peace and rest. But as soon as he turned his trust to another army, he was always troubled by war. Read those two chapters. They are great lessons on always seeking God. Put your trust in no other. Now let's check out the flag waving over your castle before your family, your job and your friends. Is it the same one you wave at church? If not go ahead, repent and tear that old flag down. Denounce any other covenants made with the enemy of your soul and get excited about your promise that there is a King living here and wave His flag. I promise you, He is a just King who forgives and provides and protects His own within

His kingdom and He loves you. Don't be a turn coat from the true family of God you are in but instead embrace His love for you. Allow Him to be King. Even if you have been saved a long time or a little time, please check your flag and do what's necessary. The last few words may seem hard but it's about such a simple truth and it's serious to our King. If it is not affecting your life like a real true King is living there, then something is wrong. Just repent and move on into His love for He loves you. He is a forgiving God that really wants to rule and reign in all of His splendor and power in your life today. So back to Jesus, Jesus, Jesus, can you see it now? As you see this, His banner of truth is flying high over your heart so all the world can see. That will make a big difference in your life, even if you have been saved forever. Walking in that revelation is life changing. It's a reason to shout and be joyful. Just think all the provision of Heaven and protection of Heaven is yours in Jesus' name! Somebody say Hallelujah.

Now that we are clear who our anointed King is and where His banner should be flying, let's look at the benefits of that. If America goes and acquires a piece of land, let's say an island for example, that is exactly what Father God did for you. He bought your relationship by the redemption price of His Son. So now the island that has been purchased is no longer under its old laws and rules nor is it under the control of who owned it. That island begins from day one to take on all the benefits of being American land, including all its technology, all its power, all its wealth, and all its health benefits. All that America has to offer in its Kingdom is now empowered to that small underdeveloped improvised island. Their money is now worth what American money is, their liberty of freedom is all in place, and they have a protective army on standby at all times. Why? Because when that land, the little island, was bought by America it received all of America's protection, and provision and prosperity. It is no longer some insignificant island but a part of the United States of America. The same is true when you accepted Jesus; you became empowered by God through Christ and now all, not leaving anything out, all of Heaven's benefits: all protection, all provision, all prosperity, all that the Kingdom of God has is now yours through Jesus Christ. Now look at what taking on the banner of Heaven does for you. It's not just some simple salvation. It's the Kingdom of God at work for you and in you so go ahead and walk around with that kind of authority. Just like the little island that was nothing now became part of a super power in the earth. You have become part of a super power over all the earth and the forces thereof. Nothing can stand against you. You wear the colors of your Father in Heaven and represent His kingdom here on earth. What an awesome thought! The super-power of all the earth abides in you.

He said, *"If ye abide in Me and My Words abide in you, you may ask whatever you will and it shall be done."* Also in John's gospel, Christ said, *"that the Father will come and dine, sup with you, and make His abode with you."* Think about it. You are the castle of the King, kind of like being the White House. Can you see yourself carrying the president in your home, and receiving all the benefits, and privileges of such. You're having all the protection that you need for you have the president with you wherever you would go. Whatever you would do would be different. Oh the power and authority that would come with such an honor. Well you have even better. The King of the world lives in you and His angels are all around you at your beck and call. His provision is yours. His protection is yours. For you house the king, you carry the Lord. What an awesome gift! What a great responsibility we have. Do we ever comprehend the magnitude of having been bought by God through Jesus Christ into His Kingdom, His deity, His authority? WOW, what a gift. I love you, Jesus.

Jesus Christ has become your conquering King. He does not just live in you, and He does not just pray before the Father for you, He does so much more. With all of His power, He goes before you and makes a way for you. Furthermore, He empowers you with His Seal of His Authority and sends you out in this world well equipped in His power and blood covenant. Now you can subdue the earth and defeat the enemies of God for His desire is to put all His enemies under His feet by His power in you. Jesus Christ, our forever Beloved King and High Priest, anoints you to be and possess the land. He waves His banner there and lets all of His enemies know that God has possessed, and lets all of His enemies know that He has possessed that ground. For the

King is here and He is in you. **Now go forth by the power of the Holy Spirit in Christ Jesus and conquer your enemies. Praise be to our God Most High!**

CHAPTER ELEVEN

FAITH: THE KEY TO UNLOCK THE (MERE) WORD

Faith, faith, faith. That's all those preaches ever say. Well, that's easy for them to say, they are out there preaching the Word every day. God seems to do more for them than the common man. And don't forget, they have all those people giving them their money, so they really don't have to have faith anyway; they have the people to bless them. Most people will not admit that they ever thought like I just wrote. Believe it or not, most people have thought like that from time to time or still think like that. All that does is undermine the power of having true faith in your life. Most people think like this. Or maybe, you personally, don't think like this. Well if it is not thinking like this, it sure is thinking in some format that is tearing down the very fiber of your faith. No matter in what form your doubt and unbelief shows up: in fear, doubt, religion, reasoning, troubles, whatever name you want to put to it, it is still undermining the power of God in your life. Faith is the supernatural key to unlock the door of possibility and the promises of God in your life to you and through you.

Where most words in the Bible are just good

stories or something that has happened for someone else, they are not that for me. Those same words, mixed and enhanced with faith, are life changing, life giving. All things are possible to them that believe in those words. But I always get this question, "Apostle Craig, what about all those people that believe in vain because what they were believing for did not come to pass?" My answer is quite simple. Even though I cannot speak for all the reasons of God, He plainly said that He asked you and me to believe that He is able and willing to do all of His Word. And His goodness will endure until the end. For when I should die, I want my confession of faith brought to the Lord as one who believed to the end. Even if I did not receive what I was believing for, I believed until the end. I do not want my confession of faith before the Lord to be as one who believed the Word and tried it out and found out that it was not true. For surely it did not come to pass when "I" wanted it to, so I have discounted the integrity of the Word of God. Now all the promises of God that I believed became to me as of no effect. You say, "Oh no, I still believe for this or that. It is just this one thing that God didn't do." Once you began to use a stopwatch on God and your faith was shattered, you began disbelieving Him in everything. Whether you can admit that or not, it is true. The Word of God becomes less powerful to you and you begin to try to trust in earthly things to take place of Godly things. Just because this didn't happen as you thought or maybe this other thing did not happen, it will sooner or later cut down the very fiber of your soul, even unto your salvation. It is impossible to please God without faith. All things are possible to them that believe. When the other is also in place, nothing is possible to those who do not believe or to those who doubt... What will it be with you, faith 100% or doubt 100%? There is no in-between. The Word said that a man who wavers is like a ship tossed to and fro in the sea, only coming to ship-wreck, not destiny. But he who believes to the end will receive the promise.

"God said it, I believe it, and that settles it!!!" What a cliché'. People say it, bumper stickers declare it, preachers preach it, and nobody really believes it. Well, maybe somebody, because there are a few exceptions. You could be one right now that's saying to yourself, "That's not true, Pastor Craig, I believe that saying." But way too often many people that say they believe that statement and confess that statement never receive the full benefit in their life. It is just another form of religious hope and wishful thinking, instead of the true revelation of what that statement of faith really means. All the power of heaven is waiting at your very word of faith to back up that statement. Jesus continually told the disciples and those who followed Him, as well as those who longed for something from Him, that it was according to their faith that they were made whole. Are you waiting on the sovereign move of God: you know where God just shows up and all is fine and you did not have to do much but receive and give thanks. Don't get me wrong, I am not saying that the sovereign move of God does not happen. But I am saying that many people miss out on the full potential of the move of God in their life because they are waiting on the sovereign move of God. Maybe He will heal us today, or maybe tomorrow. Maybe if I go over there or over to this other place, then I will receive what I need. And they go through life never getting all that was available to them by the power of the Holy Spirit and the rulership of King Jesus in their life. I'm not knocking the sovereign move of God, where He just moves no matter what you do or say. I am longing for that, but on the same hand, let it be said of me that I am walking in the fullness and all the benefits of Almighty God. I want God's power flowing in and through me that I receive all that is mine in Christ Jesus. Let's look at the man at the waters of Bethesda and how he was waiting for the sovereign move of God. For it was when the angel of the Lord would move on the waters that the first ones in would receive all that they had need of. How wonderful it was for those that were able to make it in. Oh the joy and shouting, the great rejoicing. You could hear it from all around. How troubling it must have been for those who could not get to the water edge in time to receive what they had need of. Maybe someone pushed them aside, maybe someone did not notice them , maybe someone would not help them receive all that they had need of. Is this not the case sometimes in our own churches? We get offended because we feel under-appreciated or just plain overlooked as if we were not even there. So we move on to another church only to find something else there that will hurt us or keep us from receiving all the greatness of God coming out of that ministry. You see that is the devil's plan to keep you from getting all you can from your church body. It comes, in through offense, gossip or any other lie that he feels he can get you to believe and join yourself to. It disqualifies you from receiving from that ministry source. That ministry may have just been the bread of life that would have set you free or gotten you to your destiny.

So the man sits at the waters, he can see the waters, he can smell the waters, he can even see people splashing around in the waters. From time to time a small refreshing splash splashes on him, but still, he's never getting his answer, never receiving what he needs. He is always in hope but always coming up short. Now let's get real, isn't that like us. Sometimes we go to church where the waters are and we can see the waters. We feel them as they splash us from time to time and we are so narrow minded to think we had church because we felt a little splash. We can surely smell the waters when we enter the building but way too often we never enter into the depth of what God has for us. Don't you want to know why? Most of the time it is because we are so disappointed with our faith. "Oh, no, not me, brother," you say. But if you and I would come clean for just this moment we would unlock the keys that would set us free. You see as life went on for the man at the waters even though he saw the waters, he himself had never submerged himself in those waters. He felt a splash from time to time and he could smell it and see others get into it. Therefore he was very disappointed at what his faith in those healing waters were. Maybe they healed Brother Joe or Sister Jane, but up to this point in the game of life those waters were nothing more than a side show of hope to look at. He never experienced it. So his faith got weaker and weaker. By time, he was there a little while and he was just going through the motions of being by the waters. He did not have the drive to really believe that they could or would heal him. For if he would have still believed that those awesome waters of the spirit would make him whole, you would have not been able to stop him from pressing in. Even if he would have had to crawl with his teeth, he would have made it to the edge to get his healing.

Now let's look at blind Bartimaeus. He began to cry out as loud as possible, "Jesus, thou son of David, have mercy on me. Jesus thou son of David, have mercy on me." So loud that the people around him said, "Please be quiet. You will bother the Master." But he only cried out the louder. If that happens in most churches today, that man would either be shut down or asked to leave and maybe never come back because some would think in their minds that this man is bothering the pastor or even would think he was bothering Jesus, but Jesus is not allowed to fully flow or show up in most services anyway. We have our nice little bottled up sermon and our pretty arrangement of flowers and every little thing is just in place. Dare any one to change that or interrupt that. Or God forbid that you would have to be moved by the Spirit of God to set someone free. You don't want to offend some new person that came to your church. You want them to feel comfortable, so they can come back. Hey, if they really like us, we might even get them to say a sinner's prayer and we will say people are getting saved. But in my experience, if there is no power of God then nobody is getting set free. Nobody is getting the fullness of their conversion to Christ and the rest of your people go home in the same chains that they came in with, never ever really getting set free. But you are growing and having a good time. It seems as if God's blessings and finances are growing. People are being added to your staff. Things are happening but you have not prepared Him a place to minister. You have prepared a place for you to minister in an environment subject to your liking and the people's likings. Have you ever considered God's liking and what He wanted to do in the midst of all those hurting people coming to your church? "Well," you say, "Apostle Craig, it sounds like you are speaking to pastors right now." Maybe I am but I am also talking to you, the people that make up the church, those who come in service after service not having prepared the easiest place for God to use you in, His house. Well that is what you would think, but even God finds it hard to move in His house because of unwilling people, because of people not willing to go where He wants them to go. You say, "How do you know that?" Read in the Word the life of Jesus and all the He shows us there. If most men or women of faith would begin to arise in their church like Jesus would, the leaders would probably have a coronary attack and fall out on the floor after they tried with all their might to stop the unfamiliar move of God. It is time to repent and seek God with all of our hearts and cry out to Him for His mercy and grace. Then the

Word of God will no longer be mere words on a page. They will be the expression of God's glory in the earth to you, your pastor, your church and all those around.

Now you see it was impossible to shut up blind Bartimaeus because he had heard all the stories surrounding this man Christ Jesus. He heard about how the blind see, the deaf hear, and even demons were subject to Him. He knew that he could not miss this chance to have this Man, this King, this Deity pass him by, even at the expense of his pride or ridicule from others that were trying to shut him down. "This was not going to happen," he said to himself. **"There is One here who is able to save me from this cause and I am not letting go until I get mine. I no longer want to hear about all the great stories of this Man doing for others, showing up in other people's lives, setting other people free, causing other people to receive their destiny. I can not let this moment pass**." The people began to tell him to be quiet and to shut him down. He said to himself, "You don't understand. This is Christ Jesus who is passing by. This is the Messiah. I know that this is not proper and it might not be the way my parents sought after God. My church is telling me to just be quiet and wait on some move of God or in most cases just to accept the way it is. You don't understand this is Jesus passing by." So with great vigor, he yelled only the more, "Thou son of David, have mercy on me." So much that it got the Master's attention. Jesus said, "What would you have me to do for you?" And he said,

"That I may receive my sight." Jesus said, **"Unto your faith so be it**." He was healed from that very moment. But if he would have bottled up his yell for help, held steady, waited for maybe one day when Jesus was going to come to him directly, he would have missed his opportunity to get what he needed from the Master. He might have been naturally blind but this man, above all the crowd that was around him, said he had the revelation and he knew who was there was greater than his situation. You see the people around him thought it was a bother. Like, why bother the Master with your need, you are blind now and you will be blind way after this man Jesus passes by.   But he, though blind in flesh, could see that the Son of the living God was there. And he was going to receive from Him that day. I would ask you today, do you know that the Son of the living God lives inside of you, with all the fullness and power that you and I read about in the Word of God? He has not changed. He has not weakened. He did not give up or give in to your situation. He is still very much on the throne. It is up to you and me to allow Him to be there. In your eyes go ahead and become like blind Bartimaeus. Get blinded in your fleshly eyes that you can see the glory of God with your spiritual eyes so it can manifest in your flesh.   Go ahead right now and give God the glory. You say what do you mean, He is not doing anything right now, I am just reading a book. But I tell you, if you would have eyes to see that you are not just reading a book, you are getting your eyes opened to the truth of who Jesus really is. You are seeing all the possibilities you have in Him and how much He is wanting to do for you. He loves you and He is worthy of all praise. Hallelujah!!

Faith is the revealer of the Father. The Word said it is impossible to please God without faith. Did you ever wonder what that really meant? Without faith you cannot please Him. Well you have to begin to know who He is and you can never know who He is until you begin to move into the faith realm. How can you please someone unless you know them? It's kind of like being invited to a birthday party by a friend and you really don't know the guest of honor. So you go out and buy a gift and they receive it and they appreciate it. Then you see the eyes of the guest of honor open wide with joy as he receives the gifts from his closest friends, for they knew him and were able to buy what was most precious to him. It brought him great joy and pleasure. This is kind of how the church operates, not ever getting close enough to the Lord so they don't flow in the realm of faith. Not truly knowing the heart of the Father they never fully please Him. Oh they bring a gift to the party, kind of like the invited guest. The Lord receives and likes it, but it will never please His heart like the gift of one that truly operates in faith and knows his God. It will never please Him as much as someone who knows his Father's heart, to bless Him and to receive from Him. The faith man, he leaves the party full of joy and happiness knowing that he has fulfilled his Father's wishes. He is not one that is just hoping that the Father will like the gift or accept him. He knows the mind of the Lord and how to honor and bless Him. Because it is not the ways of man or thoughts of the flesh that please the Father, it is a willing and obedient heart that will move the hand of God on your behalf. Then you can receive and do all that you are called and purposed to do.

When you start to move by faith, it begins to reveal the Father to you. You can not be contained in one salvation call or an infilling of the Holy Spirit. He has more and wants you to ever be growing into the faith of Himself. If He revealed all that He is to you at once, you would probably die right there on the spot. That is why He reveals Himself to us over a lifetime. As you walk in faith with your Heavenly Father, you will start to realize that His ways are not like man's ways. They are higher and greater. He (God) is wanting to do a lot with a little, always looking for ways to confound the wise with the least in the earth and to show forth His glory. Remember faith will always keep you one step into victory and one step away from disaster. Faith is that in which will bring you to the edge of the cliff and let you see things. Those who stay in their comfort zone will never see and go places. They will never know to go or want to go. But you and I will get to experience the Word of the Lord as more than just **_mere words on a page._**

Hebrews 10:1-10 FOR SINCE the Law has merely a rude outline (foreshadowing) of the good things to come—instead of fully expressing those things—it can never by offering the same sacrifices continually year after year make perfect those who approach (its altars). For if it were otherwise, would (these sacrifices) not have stopped being offered? Since the worshipers had once for all been cleansed, they would no longer have any guilt or consciousness of sin. But (as it is) these sacrifices annually bring a fresh remembrance of sins (to be atoned for), Because the blood of bulls and goats is powerless to take sins away. Hence, when He (Christ) entered into the world, He said, Sacrifices and offering You have not desired, but instead You have made ready a body for Me (to offer); In burnt offerings and sin offerings You have taken no delight, Then I said, Behold, here I am, coming to do Your will, O God—(to fulfill) what is written of Me in the volume of the Book. When He said just before, You have neither desired, nor have You taken delight in sacrifices and offerings and burnt offerings and sin offerings—all of which are offered according to the Law-- He then went on to say, Behold, (here) I am, coming to do Your will. Thus He does away with and annuls, the first (former) order (as a means of expiating sin) so that He might inaugurate and establish the second (latter) order. And in accordance with this will (of God), we have been made holy (consecrated and sanctified) through the offering made once for all of the body of Jesus Christ (the Anointed One).

You can clearly see that faith is the currency of heaven and it's the power that you must dwell in to achieve your purpose or promise from the Lord .

CHAPTER TWELVE

Fire in the Hole

One of the most important ingredients to the Word of the Lord becoming real in your life could be summed up in one simple but profound statement. How much *Fire in the Hole* is inside of you? Or would it be better said, 'Fire in the Whole' meaning the whole of you? How much fire of the presence of God is inside of you will help and determine how much of the Word of the Lord you have in you as well as how much Word of the Lord will come to pass in your life. You see, hearing and believing a Word of the Lord is only one aspect of getting the full potential and purpose of that Word to you. There are many key ingredients to the Word of the Lord. First of all, most people, when they get a Word of the Lord spoken over them by a prophet or pastor or any other minister or brother/sister in the Lord, will commonly make the mistake and say that it was a personal prophecy or a prophetic word. Not that it can't be but in most cases, it is a Word of Knowledge and not a prophetic Word of Prophecy. You say, "What is the difference?" Well a prophetic Word of Prophecy of the Lord will come to pass no matter what, with or without your involvement to that word. A Word of Knowledge (Don't get me wrong, a Word of Knowledge from God is no less anointed or important to you or to God) is always conditional upon many things lining up in your life or other people's lives.

I might have shared this with you before but it is worth repeating, so listen up. For example, The Word of the Lord could be that someone will give you a car. But that someone that was supposed to give you a car never lines up with God's Word and decides to try to sell you that car instead of giving you that car. Even if he gives you a great deal, he missed the opportunity of God's blessing and plan, but what was worse, he neglected the Word of the Lord to you. You never receive that Word that was spoken over you. You and many people like you have been disappointed in many of the Words of the Lord to them. In their minds, those words became just mere words on a page. It also hurts one's faith in the ministry and in believing further Words of the Lord. Because of this misunderstanding, every time somebody prophesies over you or you get a Word of the Lord in your heart and it does not come out quite the way you think it should, it causes problems with getting the Word of the Lord to materialize for you. I know what you are thinking. If God spoke it, that settles it, it will and must come to pass. Well, don't let me be the one to rattle your faith in any spoken Word from God. For I believe if God spoke it, it will and must come to pass. But in many times before, you can read in the Word, the Lord would say if you do this, then you will have this. Or if you go do this, then you will obtain that. Well, even if the Word of the Lord that was spoken over you did not come out that way, do this and I will do that, in most cases, you and many others will have to line up to His perfect plan for that matter to come to pass in the manner that you believe you will receive it. Let me give you another example of this, and this happens many of times. Say God gives you a word for ministry of some type. You are super-excited and the mood is great. Oh, how wonderful! One day soon you will be this or that and you will become this great person for God. And, oh, how joyous it will be. But then days go by or maybe months and heaven forbid years, but you know that your pastor or spiritual leader will be establishing you in the ministry of some sort. But say that pastor gets moved or leaves. Then he/she may never be able to fulfill their side of the Word of the Lord. Don't get me wrong. I don't want you to think that you can't count on the Word of the Lord. Believe me, you surely can. But it might, in most cases, take a long time or may come another way because of someone else's disobedience to the Word of the Lord.

There is also another problem with people getting so religious that they will box the Word of the Lord into happening only one way. Usually it is the way they perceived the Word when it was first given to them. But I promise you that for the most part, you and I can only see and understand in the natural realm and we will normally judge the Word in this way. But the Father may have a whole other plan in His mind. So while you are waiting for God to come and do the Word of the Lord exactly like you think, it could have passed you by in its original intended way. This will also make you think that it was just mere words on a page.

So let's go back to '*fire in the hole*.' Now I want you to think of the presence of God as a cool running river, like a fresh stream that you can see straight down to the bottom, no matter how deep it is. It's cool and refreshing. There is a light wind blowing in the background. The soft sound of the outdoors is ringing in your ears. This is how the presence of the Lord is. It is a revealer of truth and the more you hang out with it, the more you can see clearly like Him. You see it is true, you and I were made in our Father's image, but sin and life and troubles that we go through kind of beat the truth out of us. Our revealer becomes faded, weak, tattered and torn, so that we can not see as clearly as we should. This is why it is so important that you and I spend valuable time with the Lord each day (one on one). That is what He wants so very much is a people that would put a price tag on time with Him. And He wants the price tag to be so high, that it can't just be sold off by whatever comes along: the first responsibility, television or whatever it might be that you and I sell ourselves short on each and every day with our time with Him . He loves you so much and wants to accomplish so many great things in your life. If only He could be first. Because He is such a humble gentleman, He will go all day, all week, even all month waiting for you and I to come to Him and He will be patiently waiting there for us. But in that kind of relationship we never get the fullness that He intended for us. So many words go unspoken and so many desires go unmet.

You know that the Word said that we see in part and that we know in part. Well, we read the Word and study it and other times we get a personal prophecy from someone or a Word of the Lord comes to us directly, or we heard the word preached over some pulpit, and it really hits home. As much as you and I would like to think we see everything and we know what way God is telling us to go, we are only getting that information in part. Granted sometimes it is given to us in big parts, but if we are willing to be honest with ourselves and the Lord, we usually know very little in the full scheme of things that God is saying to us or how to get to this point. He does this on purpose so you and I are always in a faith mode and in a hearing and obeying mode. He does not want you so far up that road that you can't simply hear His whisper of direction. He only wants to tell you enough that you go out and fulfill that quickly. Then you have to get back on your knees and ask for more direction from headquarters. You have to stay in close communication from the Chief Himself, your Father God and Lord, through His Son, our King, Christ Jesus by the working of the Holy Spirit and Comforter, which is the very breath of God. This is why it is so critical that you just don't jump to conclusions every time you hear a Word of the Lord and get a new revelation on something, whether you agree with it or not.

This is also another problem I have seen in the church. They will hear a word preached over the pulpit or the preacher will say something that they don't agree with. You begin to judge that man /woman and or that ministry. But if you would go back to realizing that you and I only see in part at best. What was being preached or taught or said may have never pertained to you. The Father might have had a better plan with those words. Someone else may have needed to hear them for whatever reason and it did not have to agree with you or me or anyone else. But we get upset or offended and go on to another church thinking we are doing ourselves good and teaching that minister that he can't preach like that. But in reality, the Father honors him for his faithfulness to keep on going in the faith and preaching. While you, on the other hand, miss out on the other great things that God sent you there for, including receiving the fulfillment of many Words of the Lord to you. I wonder if the church will ever become more than takers from each other. Maybe you were not there at all to receive fresh revelation or revival in your soul but instead to bring it to that church or people. But once again so much is missed by selfish people we call the "church".

I can't say it enough, when you and I and the body of Christ will really begin to seek God with all of our hearts and allow His presence to have its way in us, we will be changed into His image. For He is God. I know that this chapter has went in so many different directions but that's what happens when you deal with the presence of God. It will not just touch one area of your life, it will touch the total man. All of you will become changed; a little here and a little there. But, it is bound to happen if you continue in faith toward the finish line of the race that you have begun. The more you spend time with someone, the more you will know that person. The better you get to know something, the better you will pick up on its character and shape and format and habits, likes and dislikes. This is how it is with the Word of the Lord that you have. The more time you spend with the originator of that Word, the more you will understand that Word and the more you will be able to line up with that Word. I am not saying that the Word of the Lord fully relies on you to come to pass. It is always a sovereign move of God. But you do have a lot to do with it. Once again, I must remind you that the kingdom of God is a paradox. To live you must die, to gain you must give. This seems so simple just to look at the Word of the Lord and say, "I will go do this, or I will go do that," but that is not the answer. You may think, "Well, let me see, if I put a and b together, it will make c." In most cases with the Lord, that does not work. Remember He is always looking for an obedient and hearing servant . So putting your best foot forward to accomplish His Will or His Word is not what He is saying. Putting your best seeking and hearing and obeying first is what moves the heart of the Father. It causes His will to come to pass in your life. Yes, it is true. You must hear and obey and you must follow His plan. But it is not like a plan to become a doctor: First you go to high school, then college, then med school, then once you graduate, off you go. Completion is at hand. With the Lord He might tell you one thing to get you to another thing. I am trying to say that God is not bound to some set formula, guideline or dead-line like you and I are. He could give you a Word, 'If you would like to get healed, go wash in dirty water. Or if you need to pay your taxes, go fishing.'

I guess what I remember the most is, He is

God. He will most likely take you on the course less traveled to get you to your intended destiny. ***Here is why hearing and obeying the Holy Spirit is so important and having an intimate relationship with your Heavenly Father through Christ Jesus makes all the difference in you obtaining your promise.*** Hearing and obeying and walking in the revelation of the Holy Spirit are so important to one's growth as well as getting the Word of the Lord to materialize in your life. In other words, He wants you to know Him as "Daddy" but serve Him as "God." Wow, what an awesome God and Daddy we have! He loves us enough to take us to the fulfillment of every Word in our life if we will let Him.

You might ask, "How do I get fire in the 'whole of me', does it just come?" Well, I will tell you for myself, I have found out that the Spirit of God is given freely and generously to those who will sell all that they have and give themselves completely over to the Lord. Another key , which by now I am sure that you are very familiar with, is that faith is the currency of Heaven. It is the currency of everything that you need or want.   But faith is carried on another word, 'belief', which we will talk about later. But belief is a part of faith that will move Heaven and destroy the enemies so your goal and purpose can come to pass. But it never comes alone, belief comes with a little word called "longsuffering". Don't drop the book now, but this is the key to the Word of the Lord to come to pass in your life. I think it should be spelled **LOOOONNNGGGSUFFERRING**. But we want it to be longsuffering in the short form. Now just when you thought it could not get any harder, longsuffering does not come by itself, it comes with sweet 'Ole' endurance and patience. And when these two have their way with you, you'd know that you heard the Word of the Lord, for if you endure, it will come to pass. There is a main question that you must ask yourself when you received the Word of the Lord. Will you believe that Word until it comes to pass, which in most cases can take a long, long time? The number one thing that takes most people out from ever receiving the Word of the Lord to them is the waiting game. I say 'game' loosely. It is never a game; this is your life and future that you are dealing with. I wish that it were as simple as 1, 2 and 3, Presto. Somebody spoke the Word of the Lord or you heard a word from Holy Spirit and "bam," it's there. Unfortunately it almost never comes that easily. You say, "Why?" I will tell you that in Psalm 105:19 until the time that His Word came, the Word of the Lord tried Him. This is the fuel to your success in that the Word after it has tried you and had its way with you, it will bring to pass the peaceful fruit of victory.

Endurance, a word we all wish might have never been invented, is also one of the ingredients that you and I must have to see it through to our final destiny. Ask yourself how long will I believe or will I not believe . You say that sounds stupid. Well, as stupid as its sounds, you and I will be faced with that decision many, many times in our life concerning the Word of the Lord. You could say endurance is the road map to victory. Because endurance will test everything inside of you. It will test your character, it will test your faith, and it will test your ability to believe God. In spite of the circumstances it will test you and, last but not least, it will test if you think you really heard from God. It's kind of like Noah. Let's look at him for a moment. You've got the classic old guy who built an ark to save the world from extinction . But why don't you and I look a little deeper into the story. Here is a good and just man who is well-known and liked by his community, a family man. Sure, he was very committed to his God and everybody knew this. Remember, it was not like it is today, where hardly anybody serves a god. He did not have to worry about being politically correct when he spoke. They were not telling him, "Don't talk about religion and politics." You see in his day everybody served a god or many gods, so to the world, Noah was just serving 'one of the gods'. Some of the people of that time probably served Noah's God or at least knew of Him. But to most of them, it was just another god with all of their other gods to serve. To them, it was no big deal whom Noah served as god. But one day ole Noah got a mandate from Heaven that God was sick of all of mankind and was going to wipe them off of the Earth with the exception of Noah and his family and some wild animals. Now we today, we read this as just some simple Bible story about a great man named Noah. In all reality, our very existence was hanging in the balance on this one man hearing and obeying the word of the Lord with patience and endurance. Therefore, because this one man obeyed, you and I have life today.

We think it is hard when the Lord speaks a Word to us or He reveals something to us and it didn't come to pass as fast as we would like. What do you think about Old Noah? He had to stay on course and believe God and not just for some word to come to pass that he could relate to or confirm in the Bible. He had to hold on to nothing but that spoken Word of God to him of something that seemed totally impossible. By the way, up to this point in history it had never rained before. So he had to believe past doubt, way past unbelief, he even had to go beyond his own knowledge for he had no knowledge of rain. To our knowledge, this man had never built a boat before. Before you and I presume him as building just any old boat, it was the largest ship ever built at that time, and there was one main problem, there was no water for about twenty miles. If that was not bad enough, he had no way of getting this huge boat (ship) to the nearest dock to launch. So not only was the Word impossible, it did not even make sense in the natural. Did you ever have one of those words where nobody else received it with you? And you were having a hard time believing it or making sense out of it yourself? One thing I know is true, the flesh, your earthly way of thinking, usually will never be the route that the Father takes to get you to fulfill the Word of the Lord. It almost always takes a miracle, and that only happens as your faith arises to the occasion and by faith, you complete the task at hand. Noah did not have a lot of people to pat him on the back and say, "You go for it." He didn't have friends that would stand on a scripture with him or the local traveling prophet to speak a word of conformation to him. Ole Noah just had endurance. You may never know how your obedience to God's Word to you will affect the entire world or the future of somebody else's life. But it does. Noah, just one man obeying the Word of the Lord to its fullest, stayed faithful in the midst of unbelief , despair, old age and other people not agreeing with him. Even common sense went against him, but Noah heard a Word from God and obeyed. Now you and I reap the benefits of life because of it. Wow, what a story when you look at it in detail, and see how Noah had his work cut out for him to get this job done. And if you think time runs out on the Word of the Lord, that's not true either. We usually run out on God's Word before the time of obtaining the promise. Unlike Noah, who obeyed in faith for over one hundred years, I did not say ten or one hundred days, or ten weeks or months, but I am talking more time than you and I will probably live on earth. That's right, he stayed the course and was found faithful even after a hundred years had gone by. Now that is faith that you and I should live by! Realize all the possibilities that are hanging on you and I obeying the Word of the Lord. Think about how many other people it will touch and how many areas of your life it will touch. Oh, the joy that is before the man or woman or child that would dare to receive the Word. Even better someone who will believe the Word until it comes to pass. This is all done by enduring the time that it takes for the Father to complete His Word in you. Noah was no better in his endeavor to follow God than you or I, he faced the same trials or even worse, but he saw it through to the end. You are just as able to receive the Word of God in your life as Noah was. God's word will never fail you even if people around you may fail you or try to hold you back.

The Master will never come up short. You can rely on this. You see it will always come back to your personal relationship with Christ that makes the difference. No, I am not talking about being born again. None of this really works for you if you are not born again. So I am assuming if you are hearing and obeying God, you are already a Christian. But being born again and claiming Jesus Christ as your Lord and Savior are not enough to reach destiny in the things that the Father tells you. You must walk it out, press on through, draw closer to God every day, seek Him, and get to know Him. The more you grow in Him, the more time you spend with Him, the more you will see the Word of the Lord come to pass. You will have more spiritual strength to endure as well. And the closer you get to Christ, the clearer things seem. Your spiritual eyes will open more and more. You say, "Why?" Because He promises that He is a Rewarder of those that diligently seek Him. And He loves you and desires the closest relationship with whoever will seek after Him. He is no respecter of persons, so that means His wisdom and power and might are not just reserved for the super Christian or the big time minister. It is for whoever will go after Him and find Him. You see the more you read your Word, the more you seek His face, the more you pray in the Spirit and the more you get involved in your local church and serve in the house of God, the more you set yourself up for God to move greatly on your behalf. You then get closer to the fulfillment of His Word to you, for truly His words are never ***mere words on a page.***

II Timothy 3:15-17 And how from your childhood you have had a knowledge of and been acquainted with the sacred Writings, which are able to instruct you and give you the understanding for salvation which comes through faith in Christ Jesus (through the leaning of the entire human personality on God in Christ Jesus in absolute trust and confidence in His power, wisdom and goodness). Every Scripture is God-breathed (given by His inspiration) and profitable for instruction, for reproof and conviction of sin for correction of error and discipline in obedience, (and) for training in righteousness (in holy living, in conformity to God's will in thought, purpose, and action), So that the man of God may be complete and proficient, well fitted and thoroughly equipped for every good work.

The Word of the Lord is true and our loving Father is doing all that he needs to do to accomplish His will in your life. For it is His greatest Joy to find delight and pleasure in a son or a daughter that enters into their intended destiny.

Our God is God....

CHAPTER THIRTEEN

Holy Spirit: the Revealer of Truth

Jesus said in John 14: 26, " *But the Helper, the Holy Spirit, whom the Father will send in My name, He will teach you all things, and bring to your remembrance all things that I said to you. Also John 14:16,17 "And I will pray the Father, and He will give you another Helper, that He may abide with you forever. The Spirit of Truth, whom the world cannot receive, because it neither sees Him nor knows Him; but you know Him, for He dwells with you and will be in you."* **Now,** let's go to John 16:13, *"However, when He the Spirit of Truth, has come, He will guide you into all Truth; for He will not speak of His own authority, but whatever He hears He will speak; and He will tell you things to come."* **Vs14** " *He will glorify Me, for He will take of what is Mine and declare it to you. "*

As you began to read these scriptures, it did not take long to realize that this Holy Spirit that Jesus promised us would come into the world and come upon us and live in us is a big key to unlocking the Word of the Lord. Holy Spirit will help turn something from black and white or mere words on a page to the Word of God revealed in us and moving through us. The Baptism of the Holy Spirit is one of the main keys to open up your eyes of revelation to the Word. What did Jesus call the Holy Spirit? He called Him the Spirit of Truth, a teacher of all things and a guide. And this was only the beginning. As you and I read on in the Word and study the working of the Holy Spirit, we will find that this entity called the Holy Spirit is the awesome might and power of Almighty God revealed to man. He is the third part of the God-Head: Father, Son and Holy Spirit. Wow, what a gift that Jesus promised would come after His death, burial and resurrection! Not only did Jesus promise us this incredible gift, God the Father promised it and declared it in the Old Testament. ***"That in the last days I will pour out of My Spirit on all flesh."*** The Holy Spirit was foretold for a thousand years before it ever came. This is the baptism that the Lord poured on His disciples on the day of Pentecost in Acts chapters 1-4. Jesus Christ told them not to do anything until they got this gift. My Father will pour out His spirit on you in a way that you will be submerged in the Holy Spirit and begin to have the Spirit of Truth on you and better yet, in you. Wow, what an awesome God we serve! All the keys to Heaven and Earth were now dropped down on man and now it has been revealed to you and me. So by the revelation of the Spirit of the Lord, the keys and principles of His Word can be manifested in us. What an incredible gift. I just have to take out this moment in this book and give God the praise for all He is doing in the earth and in the hearts of man. Go ahead right now and praise Him and receive the Holy Spirit. Maybe you have never received the baptism of the Holy Spirit. Well right now, call upon your God and ask Him for it. He will give it to you by faith. Right now, right where you are at, just take out this moment and receive. I'm not trying to preach doctrine or get you to change your church or even to believe another way. I just want you to receive the fullness that God said you or any believer can receive. Receive the secret code to unlocking the Bible. It is not years of study, even though that is good and necessary, and it is not a Bible degree or becoming a scholar. It is all wrapped up in having a personal relationship with the Father through Jesus Christ by the working of the promise in the Holy Spirit of God. This is the seal of the promise of eternal life. Hallelujah! Maybe you are already baptized with the Holy Spirit and you have allowed Him to become a common place, or maybe you are dull in your hearing of the Word of the Lord. Right now, I encourage you to reach out and renew your faith in the power of Jesus Christ to reveal His Word to you by the power and knowledge and gifting of the Holy Spirit of God.

The Spirit of God is always looking to show up strong in your life and reveal the truth of the Word of God. It is one of the strongest weapons against the Devil (the enemy of your soul). The enemy knows if he can keep the baptism of the Holy Spirit out of your life and out of the church, then he can beat us. You see the Holy Spirit is like the Master General of God's plan that goes out into the world to perform the will of the Father in all of our lives. But if we reject Him, smother Him or just don't tap into this gift, we all wind up on our own pages in life. We will be believing what we say is right or wrong, entrusting the salvation of our souls to what we can study, or what others may tell us instead of relying on the Spirit of Truth to reveal it to us as one church. We are called to be one body. If you read, salvation was not preached until you get to the book of Acts. You will see clearly that it still was not preached until after the baptism of the Holy Spirit was poured on the disciples in the upper room. Then Peter began to preach and over three thousand souls were added to the church. They heard the disciples speak in tongues as the Spirit of God gave them utterance. I know some of you were taught that speaking in tongues was so they could preach to the people in their own language. But that was not true. It is true that the man that heard them did understand that the words coming out of their mouths were praises to God. But nowhere in the Bible does it confirm the theory that God gave the disciples a different language just for preaching. Instead, if you do a study, you will find out that in the book of Acts, which is the first book that the known believer on Jesus' conversion began to happen, all that called on the name of the Lord and repented for their sins began to speak in tongues as the Spirit gave them utterance. Even as Peter was preaching to the Gentiles about Jesus and salvation, they began to speak in tongues. And as you read further in the New Testament, you will find out that speaking in tongues was not always understood by man. You will find that speaking in tongues is a prayer language of the Holy Spirit that only the Holy Spirit and the Father can understand. Is the Father praying His will through you? Unless there be an interpreter there, you may never know in your flesh what you just prayed for but in your spirit, you will know the mind of Christ.

Read Romans 5:5 and Romans 8:1-28. Pay close attention to Romans 8:26-28. Oh, how awesome it is to have the Word of God revealed to us by the Holy Spirit. For you see the Holy Spirit is much, much more than just speaking in unknown tongues. It is the God-given gift of revelation. We may all know that the Word of God is the very inspired Word of God to man. But you must ask yourself, inspired by what or better yet, by whom. And the answer to that question is, the Word of God was inspired by the Holy Spirit. So therefore it seems to me that it will take the Holy Spirit giving you and me the full interpretation of God's Holy Word. This is also another very important reason we need the baptism of the Holy Spirit so that you and I can continue to walk in new revelation as God, through His Holy Spirit, brings us to deeper knowledge of His Word. It gives us keys to unlock His Word. You see if the Word of God is a road map to the principles and benefits of the Kingdom of God, then the Holy Spirit is the anointed navigator.

The Word said that the Holy Spirit is a comforter, a helper, a leader of truth, and a friend that will never leave us nor forsake us.

Jesus said that He would not leave us as orphans but that He would send another and that precious gift is what we know now as the Holy Spirit of the Living God. **The third part of the God-head. The Revealer.**

CHAPTER FOURTEEN

The Final Conquest

Mere words on a page, how does it ever get that way? One day, we get the Word of the Lord and everything seems beautiful and lovely as we receive the Word with great joy and delight. But it does not take long before time passes. Oh, don't get me wrong, sometimes the Word of the Lord comes and immediately it begins to take its course in your life. Those are the awesome times that we rejoice in. Nothing seems it can go wrong and if you are anything like me, those are the times that you look for and desire every time the Word of the Lord is spoken to you or revealed to you. Just for a moment, let's take a break and give God the glory for His Word. Let's give Him thanks for every time that the Word of the Lord has come unto you. You know, here we are trying to figure it out, but in all reality His Word is awesome, His promises are 'yea, yea, and amen' to the believer.

We have a great hope in all that He said in Joshua 1:8. The Bible said, "**This Book of the Law shall not depart from your mouth, but you shall meditate on it day and night that you may observe to do according to all that is written in it. For then you will make your way prosperous**

and then you will have good success, (vs. 9) **Have I not commanded you? Be strong and of good courage do not be afraid, nor be dismayed, for the Lord your God is with you wherever you go.** Wow, what a terrific promise from God's Word. So as I just said, let's praise Him right now. Go ahead and shout the victory, you know why. Because even if you and I don't understand everything, that has no barring on the awesome power of the Holy Spirit fulfilling His Word to us. He loves us. What a gift? What a promise? Jesus will make Himself and the Father real to us. He will not lie and He will not withhold Himself or His plans from us. He will come to you and make all things new, for this is His Word to you. Shout glory be unto God. It looks like we are going to have church right here and right now for I feel the power of the Holy Spirit confirming His Word unto us. He wants us to know His will and His Word and He wants to perform it for you and me. In that we can rest. True rest comes in your praise to God, so sing, sing aloud unto your God! If you are filled with the Holy Spirit, go ahead right now and fill yourself up with Him by praying in the Holy Spirit. This enhances your understanding of this book as well as your understanding of His Word. If you are not filled with the Holy Spirit and the gifting of a spiritual prayer language, go ahead right now and receive it by faith in Jesus Christ, who is just and faithful to pour out the gift on you. Right now, receive it and if you already have it, receive a double portion of the Holy Spirit. Somebody shout "Glory" with me right now unto our Glorious King, Jesus Christ, the Great Defender of the Faith and of His

Word.

As much as I am trying to write this book right now, I feel the Holy Spirit is wanting to pour out on you something I can't write. Fresh revelation is something you can not get from a book or even from wisdom of man. He wants to give you fresh revelation from Him right now. So go ahead, wherever you are and receive it, call out to your God and He will answer. Tell Him that you want all of Him right now and He promises that He will give you all of Himself. Is He an unfaithful Father that if His son would ask for fish, He would give him a serpent? Or who of you would ask the Father for bread (the wisdom of God's Word) and He would give you a stone? No, He is saying right now if you would call out to Him, He would hear from Heaven and reveal all things unto you. So receive the peace of Jesus Christ, right now. He is also pouring the Baptism of the Holy Ghost as well as healing. Get it, get it, get it now! Be healed in the name above every sickness and disease , Jesus Christ, by the power of the Holy Ghost and by the precious Blood of the Lamb. You see the Holy Spirit can reveal the Word of the Lord more than any other thing in the world. That is why He sent Him to you to be a Comforter as well as the Spirit of Truth. So don't reject Him, you won't get far along your course without Him.

Another great key to unlocking all the possibilities of God's Word to you is the revelation of who you are in the earth as a son or daughter of the Lord Most High. You see, it is not just the written

Word of God that you and I want to come to pass in our life. But I believe more so is the importance of the ever-speaking Word of the Lord that He is saying, right now, today! A lot of times, we seem to miss God or His Word because we will either read a Word in the Bible or hear a good sermon and begin to take that Word on ourselves. And as important as it is to read your Word every day, it is just as important to go to church and sit under the anointed preaching and reactivate the Word of the Lord that is being preached to you. There is one more factor that you and I must give account for. That is the very spoken Word of the Lord God Almighty, the Word that He is speaking to us. It is way beyond a good sermon that may minister to your soul or a great scripture that may touch your heart. You must ask yourself, "What is the Father speaking to me personally? What point, rather whole or in part, of that scripture is He telling me that it is for me right now? What part of that dynamic sermon is the Father speaking to me as the Word of the Lord for me, right now at this moment?" This is the Word of the Lord that will come to pass in you and through you. When you take on the Holy Word of the Lord that was spoken to you in your spirit by the Holy Spirit, He makes it real to you. This is the one that you can bank on. For the Father is ever speaking to man in this age and giving him or her instructions on hearing and obeying His plan, that He may make known His will in the earth through that man or woman. So you and I must have a keen ear and eye to take on the awesome Word of the Lord that the Father is speaking to you directly by the Holy Spirit including when you are under a sermon or in your Word studying. The Lord will confirm to you His Word or words of that passage or sermon that is for your situation, for this time, here and now. It could be a part or the whole thing but that what He speaks and confirms to your heart in your spirit, that will be the Word that you will have to walk out and believe Him for. You will have to see it through to the end or until it comes to pass.

But first, let's look a little deeper at what the Word says on this matter of who you and I really are. Now go with me to St. John 1:1. *In the beginning was the Word, and the Word was with God and the Word was God. (vs.2)   He was in the beginning with God. (vs. 3) All things were made through Him, and without Him nothing was made. (Vs.4) In Him was Life and the Life was the light of man, (vs. 5) and the light shines in the darkness, and the darkness did not comprehend it. (Vs.. 6) There was a man sent from God, whose name was John.*

As you look at these scriptures you will easily see that the writer is talking about our wonderful Savior and conquering King, Jesus Christ. But is that all that there is to these scriptures or could they be saying a lot more. Jesus, through His Word, was trying to unlock one of the biggest mysteries of man and to get this revelation of who we are to the Father and to the world out to us. And if you look really deep into these scriptures, you will clearly begin to see the ultimate promise of God that you and I can stand on. Even if what I am about to tell you sounds familiar, don't take it that way because religious thinking and just plain old natural thinking won't get it. You need to put on the eyes of the Spirit of God. Jesus was in the beginning with God. He was God and is in God but He Himself lowered Himself to an earthly state of man to become the Word in the flesh, for many reasons, yes, but one that we can't overlook. The Word also says that Jesus was the first of many brethren. He was the second Adam, a perfect creation without sin. Even so He was tempted in all ways but He did not sin. Wow! So He made a way that you and I will be joint heirs (equal heirs) with Christ unto God. That's right, you and I are sons and daughters of God Almighty. Well, you probably are saying, "What is so profound about that? I've been told that my whole Christian life." This is true but being told something and walking in its full revelation are two different things. Most Christians will agree with me and say, "That's right, Pastor Craig, I am a son or daughter of God." There is so much more to it than that. Most Christians are not living in the fullness of the benefits of that promise because until it becomes revelation that you and your words and your actions represent God in the earth, you will not get all that God has for you. Think about it, all the power of the universe in Christ is inside of you. The Father, the greatest being that ever existed, has made existence inside of you. The One with no beginning and no end lives in you and His Spirit dwells with you! What can come against the child of God that walks in this knowledge and uses the power that God gives them to put this earth and the devil and all of life's trials into submission under the authority of Christ that is within them? Nothing. You and I , we are the living breathing moving Word of God in the earth , just like Christ was. Don't get me wrong I am not saying that we are the Deity, but I am saying that Jesus is now made flesh in you and me. The Father now walks among man, through us and we are His manifestation in the earth. What an awesome responsibility that God entrusted us with! You have the power of life and death in your mouth; you can cause blessing or cursing. The Spirit, I mean exactly the same Spirit that rose Jesus Christ from the dead with resurrection power, is the same Spirit that the Word says now lives in you. Do you know what that means and what and who that makes you? A true real-life expression of the glory of God is what it makes you. Our God is just waiting for you to arrive to this knowledge in Him and begin to walk in this revelation and take control of the world around you, bind what needs to be bound and loose what needs to be loosed. Cause the world to come under the authority of Christ that is in you. You do want the Word of the Lord to come to pass, don't you? Go out and declare God's will to this world and subdue your enemy, the devil, and win this battle. For you have the victory because the one who already won this war lives in you and me and has redeemed us back in to full relationship with God. This makes us true sons and daughters with all the benefits and power and authority. Now therefore, you Christians, the called of God, it's time for you to arise and take over the enemy of God and put your life in order and reach your destiny in Christ.

There is a mandate from heaven. Can you not hear the strong voice of the Lord calling out? It is like a summertime dinner bell in an open field, so all may hear. "Come, come to the table of the Lord. Arise my sons and daughters and take your place in heavenly places here on earth by the power and revelation of the Holy Spirit. Do you not believe, can you not perceive? The wealth of this world is **Mine**, the health of life is **Mine**, the beauty of fulfilled destiny is **Mine**, and I give it to my sons and daughters so they may triumph over their enemy's head. Remember, he is My enemy too. Anyone or anything that has risen up against you, I will destroy. My Word says, *'Touch not my anointed nor do them any harm.' Trust in me,"* saith the *Lord of Hosts.*

CHAPTER FIFTEEN

The Restoration and the Redemption of His Love

Romans 8:1 *There is therefore now no condemnation to them which are in Christ Jesus, who walk not after the flesh, but after the spirit. (vs. 7) Because the carnal mind is enmity against God; for it is not subject to the law of God, neither indeed can be. (vs. 9) But ye are not in the flesh, but in the Spirit, if so be that the Spirit of God dwell in you. (vs. 10) And if Christ be in you, the body is dead because of sin, but the Spirit is life because of righteousness. (vs. 11) But if the Spirit of Him that raised up Jesus Christ from the dead dwell in you, He that raised up Christ Jesus from the dead shall also quicken your mortal bodies by His Spirit that dwelled in you. (vs. 14) For as many as are led by the Spirit of God, they are the Sons/Daughters of God (vs. 15) For you have not received the spirit of bondage again to fear, but you have received the spirit of adoption whereby we cry "Abba Father" (vs. 16) The Spirit Himself bears witness with our spirit that we are children of God, (vs. 17) and if children, then heirs of God and joint heirs with Christ if so be that we suffer with Him, that we may be also glorified together. (vs.18) For I reckon that the sufferings of this present time are not worthy to be compared with (the restoration) the glory which shall be revealed in US.*

You may wonder why I am writing this to you in this last small chapter in the book. I call this the final icing. We know according to Romans 10: 17 *that faith cometh by hearing and hearing by the Word of God.* And also in chapter 10 vs. 10 *for with the heart man believeth unto righteousness ; and with the mouth confession is made unto salvation and in vs. 13 of the same chapter; For whosoever shall call upon the name of the Lord shall be saved* . You and I will never come to the fullness that God the Father has for us if we don't come into the revelation of whom and what we became at the moment of our conversion as believers.

Let's look a little further in His Holy Word. Revelations 22: 12 says *And behold, I come quickly; and My reward is with Me, to give every man according as his work shall be. (vs.13) I am Alpha and Omega, the Beginning and the End, the First and the Last.*

"I dwell in the hearts of man, and I am more than able to show myself strong for I am the Lord thy God. Serve Me with all of your

heart. Put down your golden idols, put down your religious attributes and your prejudice, and allow Me to do My mighty work among My people. For I am a jealous God, do you not see how I gave My all in My love to make a way for you? You and I shall be one for eternity. Stop thinking in the now only. Yes, I am a God of the now, but I change not and I am planning your future for millions of years to come if you can receive this. I write things on your heart that no one has ever heard before. Get out of religion and follow Me to the plan that I have for you. Let Me breathe My Spirit on you. Give way to My anointing and let Me do all that My Spirit has intended to do. For I am a jealous God for My people who are hungry for Me. Give them all of Me, do not any longer hold back that which is Mine for I have a lot to give to the believer who is willing to draw more from Me and believe Me for more. All of My secret places and thoughts of heaven will lead your pathway," said the Lord.

Wow, what a God that He would interrupt the writing of this book to talk to us directly with His Spirit. He longs so much to do great things in your life. Let's look at Revelations 22: **14 Blessed are they that do His commandment, that they may have the right to the tree of life and may enter in through the gates into the city.** He is talking about us and the city is His. Sometimes I think we forget about this place. This is a place where because of His Amazing Grace and love you and I will glorify Him for eternity. Let that sink in for a moment and see if that doesn't help you see things a little clearer. Yes, our awesome God is in the here and the now but He also wants us to realize this is only one phase of our existence with Him. We have been made in His image, meaning that we are eternal, and we shall rule and reign with Him forever. We shall declare His Glory for millions of years. So it does not matter what the devil said or what the world said. It doesn't matter about any other obstacles in your life. The Word of the Lord is true and will accomplish all that it was intended to do, whether we see it or not. Sometimes that Word is not sent to accomplish what you think you heard or believed that it is supposed to accomplish. It may be the nudge that will take you from one glory to another glory or from one victory to another victory. Even though, it may never come out like you and I think, God is in control. He knows what He's doing.

Let's look at the movie "The Karate Kid." His teacher told him, "Wax on. Wax off." Showing him how to clean a car was the way he was teaching him karate. The karate kid could have rebelled or began to doubt his teacher or just blown it off. He could have tried something else or tried to find another way or worse yet, another teacher. Then he would have missed the ultimate goal of all, learning exactly what he needed and receiving the prize of the highest rank. But it did not come the way he thought. That is how we need to be. We need to trust our teacher, Jesus Christ. Judging the Word or God Himself will only delay or cause that Word not to happen. Hearing and obeying the Word of the Lord without question or hesitation is so important. It should be our proclamation . We need only be moved by the Word of the Lord, not our flesh or our emotions or our offenses, but by the Spirit of the Lord.

The Father loves you so much. Right now take a new look at His love for you. I don't care how long you have been a Christian, receive His love afresh right here, at this moment. Let Him forgive you of every sin or shortcoming in your life. Let His joy flood over you. You are forgiven and you are righteous! I promise you will never overcome sin in your life or get true control over vices, habits and other problems until you realize His awesome love and grace and His wonderful mercy that endures forever through Christ Jesus. You are not condemned, you are not a sinner saved by grace. Better yet, it is that grace that has made you and me free to receive all of the benefits of the Kingdom of God and move on in the things of God. You must see yourself made perfect in Christ Jesus, because the Father sees you as clothed with salvation. He put His robe of righteousness (right-standing with God) on you. Until you see yourself as a joint heir of Christ, equally redeemed by the blood of His covenant, you will be hard pressed to see the fulfillment of all of the Word of the Lord to you. Right now, I just want to take a moment to erase condemnation from the believer. If you are battling with sin, then ask our awesome Father to forgive and receive His wholeness and redemption. Know that you are righteous. The devil is a liar. That sin in your life or that problem will not be the last of you, because He went to a cross and paid for your sins, troubles and sicknesses. He paid them in full and He has it all under control. So lay down the doubt of your faith and believe that the Word of the Lord is more than mere words on a page. They are life and they were given to you that you would arise as a son or daughter in the earth dressed in all of His power and glory. For He loves you and our God is God. I pray that the writing of this book has encouraged you and given you freedom to hear and obey and believe the Father at His Word and to trust in Him until the time of the fulfillment comes.

Yours in Him

Apostle Craig N. Wells

Chapter Sixteen

Why an Apostle?

This is a question that many people have asked, or better yet, the real question at hand. How are you an apostle? Did not the apostles die out with Matthew, Mark, Luke and John? By what right or authority do you call yourself an apostle? Someone once said, "Who died and left you king?"

So, let's cut through all the red tape and inquiries and let's get right down to the point. Why an apostle? Well, first of all, you and I must come to the understanding of what God the Father is doing in this time for the church. He is reestablishing His five-fold ministry and authority of His church on the earth. I did not call myself to be or make myself an apostle. This call is no different than the call of God on your life; whether you are called to be a teacher, preacher, pastor, evangelist, or you could be called to be a deacon or bishop or in the helps ministry of some sort. Maybe your call is a business man or school teacher, but no matter what the call of God is on your life, we must remember, *it is the call of* **GOD.** So God the Father, in His awesome wisdom, calls us according unto His will and He has called me to be an apostle. It is like a pastor or evangelist or any other call by God. It's just a different function of the government of God's leadership.

Let's go to Ephesians 4:11 *"**And he (being***

*God) gave some to be **Apostles**; and some Prophets; and some, Evangelists; and some Pastors and Teachers; (vs. 12) For the perfecting of the saints for the work of the ministry, for the edifying of the body of Christ; (vs. 13) Till we all come into the unity of the faith. And of the knowledge of the Son of God, unto a perfect (mature) man, unto the measure of the stature of the fullness of Christ."* Also, let's look at **Ephesians 2:19-20** *Now, therefore, you are no more strangers and foreigners, but fellow citizens with the saints and you are of the household of God; and you are built upon the foundation of the **apostles** and prophets, Jesus Christ, Himself, being the chief cornerstone.*

You can easily begin to see here that God has sent His apostles and prophets as well as His pastors, evangelists and teachers to establish His church on a solid foundation that they may grow unto maturity. You will also see that the church was established on the foundation of the apostles and prophets, and I believe that God is still doing that today. I have a little slogan at our church. "We are the church of the future, back from the past." Don't get me wrong, we are not going back into old-time religion and spiritual junk. But we are moving onward with the establishment of the government of God that he started the church out with. He has never changed His mind! All of the functions of the ministry are so important to the church as a whole. How great is the function of the evangelist to bring man to Christ and Christ to man. And we have learned in the last decades how invaluable it is to have the function of great teachers to lead us into new truth and revelation of God's Word. How awesome it has been to be able to receive the function of the prophetic Word of the Lord, of wisdom and encouragement, from the modern-day prophets. And what a gift that we have in the churches of the world today as we have been nurtured and cared for by the function of our pastors, but now is the time that God is bringing back the fullness of His Headship in the church through apostolic order (apostles) that He set forth.

In Ephesians, He called out His apostles. Now, once again, He is calling them out to take their places in the church of the Lord Jesus Christ. And together ***Apostles, Prophets, Evangelists, Pastors, and Teachers*** will bring the fullness of God and the unity of the church into its intended form of a mature man, in the image of God by Christ Jesus, full of the power of the Holy Spirit.

I would like to say thank you for investing into this book, and I pray that it has ministered to you in such a way that you have the strength and the faith to see the Word of the Lord through to the end. That you may obtain all the promises of God for your life is my prayer. And, as I heard a great man say, "I'll meet you at the finish line." Until then, may you continue to prosper and grow in the things of God all the days of your life...

Apostle Craig Nathan Wells

Notes....

To Contact The Author, Write:

Rock World Ministries
P.O.BOX 490
Slidell, LA. 70459
Or Call: (985) 639-3456

Internet Address:
www.rockworldministries.com

Also for speaking engagements with
Apostle Craig N. Wells
You may E-mail him at
apostlecwells@wmconnect.com
You may write or call the address & phone number above

To find out more information about
The Rock Church of Greater New Orleans
You may look us up on the web at
www.rockworldministries.com

When writing us or e-mailing us please enclose any testimony or help
that you might have received from this book or ministry.
All prayer requests are welcomed.

Mere Words On A Page

Book re-order form

For additional copies of this book please mail a check to:

ROCK WORLD MINISTRIES
P.O.BOX 490
SLIDELL. LA. 70459

written out to: The Rock Church
In the amount of your total order plus shipping and handling per book.
1 book for $20.00
2 books for $30.00
Each additional book after two books is $15.00 each
Add $3.95 shipping & handling for the first book
Then add $2.50 for each additional book that you order .
These books will be sent out to you within ten days of receipt of your check.

Once again Thank You for the opportunity of speaking into your life. Be blessed always.